Poverty in South Africa
Past and Present

JACANA POCKET SERIES

The new series of Jacana pocket guides is meant for those who are looking for a brief but lively introduction to a wide range of topics of African history, politics and biography, written by some of the leading experts in their fields.

Already published

Steve Biko
(by Lindy Wilson)
Shaka
(by Dan Wylie)
Govan Mbeki
(by Colin Bundy)
South Africa's Struggle for
  Human Rights
(by Saul Dubow)
South Africa at War, 1939–45
(by Bill Nasson)
The ANC Women's League
(by Shireen Hassim)
The Soweto Uprising
(by Noor Nieftagodien)
Ingrid Jonker
(by Louise Viljoen)
Umkhonto weSizwe
(by Janet Cherry)
San Rock Art
(by J.D. Lewis-Williams)
Plague, Pox and Pandemics
(by Howard Phillips)

The ANC Youth League
(by Clive Glaser)
The Idea of the ANC
(by Anthony Butler)
Short-changed: SA since
  Apartheid
(by Colin Bundy)
Chris Hani
(by Hugh Macmillan)
Patrice Lumumba
(by Georges Nzongola-
  Ntalaja)
Thomas Sankara
(by Ernest Harsch)
Haile Selassie
(by Bereket Habte Selassie)
Nelson Mandela
(by Colin Bundy)
Frantz Fanon
(by Christopher J. Lee)
Jack Simons
(by Hugh Macmillan)

Poverty in South Africa
Past and Present

A Jacana
pocket history

Colin Bundy

First published in southern Africa by
Jacana Media (Pty) Ltd in 2016

10 Orange Street
Sunnyside
Auckland Park 2092
South Africa
+2711 628 3200
www.jacana.co.za

ISBN 978-1-4314-2412-2

Published in the United States and United Kingdom by
Ohio University Press, Athens, Ohio

Cover design by publicide
Set in Minion 10/14.5pt
Printed by Creda Communications
Job no. 002816

See a complete list of Jacana titles at www.jacana.co.za

Poverty in South Africa
Past and Present

A Jacana
pocket history

Colin Bundy

First published in southern Africa by
Jacana Media (Pty) Ltd in 2016

10 Orange Street
Sunnyside
Auckland Park 2092
South Africa
+2711 628 3200
www.jacana.co.za

ISBN 978-1-4314-2412-2

Published in the United States and United Kingdom by
Ohio University Press, Athens, Ohio

Cover design by publicide
Set in Minion 10/14.5pt
Printed by Creda Communications
Job no. 002816

See a complete list of Jacana titles at www.jacana.co.za

Contents

Introduction

'Poverty is death in daily episodes'
 — Mir Taqi Mir, classical Urdu poet

Poverty is material want, shabbiness, and squalor. Clothes patched beyond repair; shoes literally down-at-heel; bedding stained and worn thin; furniture and fittings that sigh with exhaustion. Poverty is housing without the basic amenities, comforts or security that home life is supposed to afford. Urban poverty is space so cramped that privacy is impossible: shacks that leak when it rains, swelter in summer, and freeze in winter; candles and paraffin heaters and the fire hazards these present.

Poverty is the infection caused when the hookworm parasite burrows into the intestine of a child. Or any one of the other diseases transmitted by contaminated water or by contact with human faeces: gastroenteritis (in the 1980s, still the biggest cause of death in South Africa's coloured population), dysentery, typhoid, cholera.

Poverty is malnutrition: not just the pangs of hunger when food is short in the home – although poverty is hunger too – but the long-term, endemic condition caused by poor or inadequate diet. Malnutrition hits children hardest. It deprives young bodies of the proteins, vitamins, carbohydrates and variety required for healthy growth; and it announces its presence on the body: stunted growth, bleeding gums, roughened or discoloured skin, and sores that refuse to heal. Malnutrition dulls young minds, making it difficult to concentrate; it saps energy, leaving children listless and distracted, performing poorly. Exactly these symptoms were described when the Carnegie Commission investigating the 'Poor White question' took evidence in the early 1930s.[1] Precisely similar findings have been reported countless times in recent decades in the literature on impoverished African schools.

Poverty prompts desperate measures. Acute shortages can turn people into scavengers, beggars and thieves. Being deprived of goods or leisure or security means that when alcohol or other drugs are available, poor people may abuse them ferociously. Poverty creates stress and stress triggers violence. In South Africa, as in other societies, poverty makes domestic violence (especially violence against women) more frequent and severe.[2] Extreme poverty forces individuals and entire communities into the dystopic state of nature envisioned by Hobbes. He held that without a social contract, life was 'poor, nasty, brutish, and short': for those living in acute poverty, this is a statistically accurate prediction.

Poverty diminishes people, leaving them powerless to shape their lives. Poor people have less ability to make meaningful choices and to act on them; their autonomy is pinched and compromised. They are thrust to the margins of their society; their needs ignored, their human worth discounted. Yet poverty also generates countless instances of resilience and adaptation. Very poor people summon up, time and again, ingenuity, determination and unquenchable hope. Navigating shoals of misfortune and want, they make homes, invent new urban forms, and find ways of sustaining their families. Poverty is a chronicle of suffering; it is also a saga of survival.

* * *

More prosaically, poverty is also a field of inquiry. Poverty is studied especially by economists, sociologists and historians – but also by scholars from a range of other disciplines. Such inquiry and study produce what Grace Davie has called 'poverty knowledge': that is, 'public representations of material deprivation and inequality that inform, and are informed by, scientific research'.[3] For anyone writing about poverty, Davie provides a salutary warning in describing the elusive, slippery and ambiguous nature of poverty knowledge. Scholarly analysis of poverty, she writes, oscillates between quantitative and qualitative methods of observation, creating tensions between 'statistics and stories, numbers and voices, large-scale surveys and fine-grained ethnographies'. This means that no single account 'can ever claim to be definitive given the historic and ongoing tensions between insider knowledge and outsider knowledge'.[4]

Peter Alcock agrees. In a discussion based mainly upon poverty knowledge in Britain, he points out that 'there is no one, correct, scientific, agreed definition' of poverty. This is because poverty is a political concept and inherently a contested one. Debates about its meaning 'are inextricably bound up with debates about what, if anything, to do about it'.[5] Yet some basic definitions of terms used by scholars of poverty are necessary. Most studies of poverty, in order to differentiate the poor from the non-poor, use income as a measure. Much of the work on measuring poverty (going back to classic studies in the late 19th century) has been quantitative, and has relied on one or other notion of a *poverty line* or minimum income standard. To oversimplify: such poverty lines are based either on a 'budget' of standard necessities or on a 'deprivation index' – a list of key indicators of standard of living, the lack of which is evidence of poverty – or on some combination of these.[6] Those living below a poverty line thus constructed are defined as impoverished.

In South Africa, the work of Edward Batson in devising a *poverty datum line* (PDL) in the late 1930s was extremely influential. Batson claimed that his PDL was an objective measure of the minimum amount of income that an urban family required in order to pay rent, and to purchase such food, clothing, heating and lighting materials that would permit the household to live in 'health and decency'. His work was important in that it 'announced that all human beings shared the same basic requirements'.[7] Most of the contemporary measures of poverty in South Africa – a plethora of poverty lines, household survey data, and enumerations of income and resources – derive from this approach. Like Batson's, these poverty lines are socially constructed rather than scientifically objective.

One of the major developments in poverty studies in recent decades has been an emphasis on *deprivation* instead of or, more usefully, alongside measurements of income. This approach stresses that poverty is a multi-dimensional phenomenon. Such scholarship is echoed in the Copenhagen Statement: 'Poverty has various manifestations, including lack of income and productive resources to ensure sustainable livelihoods; hunger and malnutrition; ill-health; limited or lack of access to education and other basic services; increased morbidity and mortality from illness; homelessness and inadequate housing; unsafe environments and social discrimination and exclusion.'[8]

My approach in the chapters that follow is pre-dominantly qualitative. This is partly because as an

11

historian I am more at home with analysing how societies change over time than I am at measuring such changes. It is also partly because for most of the period covered reliable statistical data are scant. This is particularly the case when it comes to measuring or calibrating the poverty of black South Africans. 'One of the attributes of the poor', Diana Wylie observes, 'is that they are not counted.' In South Africa, until late in the 20th century, 'no one computed the national rates of infant and adult mortality, fertility, nuptiality, or causes of death for black South Africans'.[9]

This dearth of data has changed dramatically, as a direct consequence of political change in South Africa. Jeremy Seekings and Nicoli Nattrass note that since the early 1990s 'extraordinarily rich data' on poverty have been produced, stimulating 'an explosion of quantitative research'.[10] Chapters 6 and 7 below draw directly on the survey materials and a plethora of statistical findings. But a proliferation of data yields neither consensus nor clarity. Poverty knowledge in post-apartheid South Africa remains highly contested and contentious. 'There cannot be many places in the world', Mark Gevisser wryly notes, 'where a bottom line is so contested – by people, no less, who share the same struggle mythology and claim to be in alliance'![11]

This book provides an historical overview of poverty in South Africa. Poverty, of course, is not a uniquely South African experience. The social and economic exclusion of the poor occurs in very many countries, and has been a feature of human societies throughout recorded history. In South Africa, at the risk of be-labouring the obvious, it has a distinctive dimension. Historically, powerlessness, vulnerability and disregard have been colour-coded. South African poverty has been profoundly racialised by legislation, by social practice, by systematic discrimination, and by deep-seated prejudices.

But racial prejudice and discrimination only ever exist within specific historical contexts. In South Africa poverty has been stamped by forms of racial discrimination shaped successively by the Dutch colonial presence and slavery, by British imperialism and wars of conquest, and by an advanced, capital-intensive, mining-based, industrial revolution in the last quarter of the 19th century. The explosive growth of capitalism and urbanisation in a colonial context shaped a set of home-grown institutions and social relations: 'native reserves', migrant labour, pass laws, job reservation, urban segregation, and the like. Poverty in South Africa was deeply affected by patterns of racial discrimination but also by the specific trajectory of class formation and exploitation. Especially for the 20th century, the concept of racial capitalism retains explanatory force in considering the history of poverty.[12] It suggests that capitalism, as it has developed in South Africa, entrenched both white wealth and privilege, and black exploitation and poverty. The development of capitalism always proceeds unevenly, but in the South African case the skewing of its costs and benefits was along a markedly racial axis.

* * *

Poverty, like any other human phenomenon, has its own history. Poverty has causes and consequences; it changes over time; and its past shapes its present. The chapters that follow argue that it is impossible to think coherently or constructively about the triple challenge of poverty, inequality and unemployment in contemporary South Africa without a clear sense of their formation. They insist that poverty in South Africa is not a natural, or a given, condition. All the most familiar aspects of poverty – queues of unemployed work-seekers, beggars at street corners, young people flooding from impoverished countryside to impoverished squatter camps, family members living off the pensions or social grants of others – are historically formed. The historical overview attempted in this book necessarily involves considerable compression and the loss of some nuance and detail. There is a great deal of ground to be covered, so here is a brief route map of the terrain.

Chapter 1 begins by outlining the nature of poverty in the precolonial past. It demonstrates, firstly, that the notion of precolonial African societies so egalitarian that no poverty existed is simply wrong; and, secondly, that patterns of accumulation and poverty were far from static or unchanging in those societies. It proceeds to explore how poverty was shaped by slavery and trekboer expansion during the Dutch colonial period; and examines the immediate and long-term implications for poverty of colonial wars and dispossession during the British colonial 19th century. The most crucial change of the closing decades of the 19th century was that urban whites, settler farmers and African subsistence farmer-pastoralists became effectively 'integrated into one single, rapidly modernizing economy and would continue to be irrevocably bound together'. Central to this process was 'the incorporation of the African people to provide the indispensable labour for a modern economy'.[13]

Chapter 2 explores the creation of what was called 'the Poor White problem' or 'the Poor White question'. It demonstrates that although there had been substantial numbers of poor settlers and colonists from the 18th century onwards, it was only in the 1890s that anxieties crystallised around the concept. In that decade, white poverty was perceived differently, and identified as the Poor White question. The Union of South Africa, created in 1910, inherited a set of anxieties about the rapid proletarianisation of rural whites and their movement in substantial numbers into city slums. The political answers to the Poor White question, forged during the 1920s and 1930s, had far-reaching implications for the

15

rest of the 20th century; they helped shape the nature and extent of poverty among the black majority.

Chapter 3 outlines what one might justly call the 'Poor Black problem' in the first half of the 20th century. It stresses key features of the South African economy: large-scale labour migration to mines and industries, and its corollary, rural 'reserves' forced to export labour in order to subsist. Chronologically, the chapter is concerned with black poverty *before* 1948 and the onset of apartheid. There is no watertight line between urban and rural poverty. Families had members who experienced both, and migrant labour impelled men from rural poverty to work in low-waged urban poverty. However, here and in subsequent chapters the forms of poverty that emerged in the countryside (both in the reserves and on white-owned farms) are considered separately from those that developed in towns and cities. A central finding is that poverty was visited with particular ferocity upon Africans in rural areas. Rural poverty has historically been more pervasive and more difficult to escape than urban poverty.

Chapters 4 and 5 review some quite startling changes in the nature of poverty during the four decades of apartheid. The 1950s saw segregation en-trenched and extended; a drive to eliminate 'squatters' and shantytowns; and the commencement of the con-struction of 'new model townships' – Soweto is the prototype – on a massive scale. On white-owned farms, this decade saw the use of cheap prison labour reach its peak. In the reserves there was a half-hearted attempt to address the economic deterioration identified by the Tomlinson Commission by accelerating 'betterment schemes'. In the 1960s and 1970s, new forms of poverty were in large degree the consequence of state policies and actions. Having failed to stem the influx of Africans to the cities, the National Party government resorted instead to expelling large numbers of the urban African population. Such social engineering created an artificial population growth in the reserves or Bantustans, exacerbating poverty levels there. These policies also generated 'displaced urbanisation', the concentration of millions of black South Africans in vast rural slums. Acute poverty was also experienced by farm workers and their families, large numbers of whom were displaced either by the accelerating mechanisation of farm work or by the government's concerted effort to expunge any remaining tenancies, sweeping away the last vestiges of an African peasantry living on white-owned land.

But by the late 1970s and the 1980s, rural and urban poverty (mainly in the form of informal settlements) intensified not so much as the result of policy as of a failing economy and major changes within the labour market. Employers who for decades had relied on cheap, unskilled labour now tried to increase production through mechanisation and the employment of more highly skilled workers. Earnings for urban 'insiders' rose significantly, but were affordable because employers were shedding unskilled and semi-skilled workers in the hundreds of thousands. There was an historic shift from labour shortages to a labour surplus – which translated directly into mass, structural unemployment. Work-seekers unable to find jobs rose from about 180,000 in the mid-1970s to over 4 million by the 1980s and perhaps as many as 6.3 million by the mid-1990s. Mass poverty rooted in mass unemployment was thus a crucial element of the legacy inherited by the ANC from four and a half decades of apartheid rule.

Chapters 6 and 7 explore the responses of successive ANC governments to that grim legacy. They do so in two different ways. Chapter 6 is a case study, focusing on one element of the ANC's policies and practices: its programmes of social welfare. The ANC has carried out a remarkable expansion of welfare provision. In 1993, about 3 million people received pensions or social grants. By 2016, pensions and grants reached almost 18 million people, or one in three South Africans. Welfare cash transfers have arguably been the most effective mechanism of redistribution used by the ANC. And yet the senior leadership of the ANC is fearful that welfare may create dependency on the state, and warns against creating a culture of entitlement. The major shortcoming of the social security net is that it has replicated welfare systems which assume full employment: it was not designed to provide for the long-term unemployed.

Accordingly, the long-term unemployed, especially young men, are almost entirely excluded from the system of welfare grants.

Chapter 7 examines the record of the ANC's 'war against poverty' more broadly.[14] When it took office in 1994, the party led by Mandela viewed combating poverty as an immediate political imperative. 'Attacking poverty and deprivation', pronounced the Reconstruction and Development Programme, 'must ... be the first priority of a democratic government.' Yet how effectively was this priority addressed? To stay with the metaphor: the ANC government has waged an attritional trench warfare, fighting foes on three linked fronts: poverty, inequality and unemployment. The modest gains it has made in reducing poverty have been offset by a failure to take any ground on the other two fronts. In 2008, a critic broadly sympathetic to the ANC voiced exasperation. The ANC had failed adequately 'to conceptualise and attack poverty'; after nearly a decade and a half in power, the party lacked 'an official anti-poverty strategy, targets, or target groups'. Its conviction that economic growth was a rising tide that would lift all boats was unfailingly optimistic but empirically dubious.[15] Nearly a decade later, this critique remains pertinent.

The chapter concludes by asking what policy options are available to any South African government trying to reduce poverty, unemployment and inequality. To what extent are domestic solutions to this triad of challenges compromised by the prevailing logic of globalised capitalism? Can an ANC government simultaneously serve the interests of Black Economic Empowerment capitalists, black middle-class professionals, workers who are typically skilled and unionised – *and* the unemployed and the poor? If unemployment – obviously – keeps people poor, what realistic prospects are there for more successful public works programmes or other forms of job creation? Any positive answer to such questions will require a political solution, not a technical one. There would have to be a realignment of political forces that would make a fundamental policy shift possible – one that seeks structural solutions to structural problems.

1

Precolonial and colonial poverty

> '... Africa's splendour lies in its suffering. The
> heroism of African history is to be found not in
> the deeds of kings but in the struggles of ordinary
> people against the forces of nature and the
> cruelty of men.'
>
> – John Iliffe

This book provides an overview of the history of poverty in South Africa. It does so, firstly, because that history – following John Iliffe – is important in its own right, reconstructing the suffering and struggles of the poor. It does so, secondly, because it is impossible to understand contemporary poverty without a sense of its origins, its long-term development and its changing character over time.

The history summarised in these pages is focused for the most part upon the period since the formation of the Union of South Africa, in 1910. But this more recent past was not written upon a blank slate. Precolonial and especially colonial forms of poverty were essential building blocks for 20th-century society; their legacy helped shape segregation and apartheid; and it persists in the post-apartheid era. So this chapter deals briefly with the earlier history of poverty in the area that is today South Africa – the history of precolonial peoples and of the first two centuries of the colonial period. The main arguments of this chapter are summarised below.

- Firstly, it dispels any notions of an idyllic precolonial past, a romantic Merrie Africa. It is sometimes suggested that early African societies were egalitarian; that the extended family provided protection against want; and that people lived in balance with nature so that they did not lack food or shelter. These are only partially accurate claims: precolonial African societies had their own forms of poverty.

- Secondly, a history of South Africa between the mid-17th century and the mineral discoveries of the late 19th century reveals entire categories of poverty created and defined by the colonial encounter. These included slavery and its aftermath; various forms of unfree labour on trekboer farms; the conquest and dispossession first of the Khoi and then of the Xhosa during the frontier wars; and patterns of differentiation within settler society, both rural and urban.

- Thirdly, it is clear that between about 1760 and the 1830s, significant changes took place within African societies that were still independent of colonial rule, but were affected in various ways by forms of interaction between indigenous peoples, settlers, slavers and traders. These changes had political and socio-economic consequences and they accentuated patterns of dependency and poverty in African polities.

- Fourthly, the discovery of diamonds and gold dramatically accelerated social, economic and political changes in the late 19th century; and shaped processes and institutions – 'native reserves', migratory labour, closed compounds, and segregated urban spaces – all of which predated 1910. Their existence profoundly affected the nature and extent of poverty in subsequent decades.

Poverty in precolonial South Africa

Knowledge of the precolonial inhabitants of the region that is today South Africa has been transformed by scholarship in recent decades.[1] The earliest dwellers were the San, or Bushmen: hunter-gatherers, living in very small-scale communities or bands, who occupied parts of southern Africa for some 10,000 years. About 2,000 years ago, they were joined by the stock-keeping Khoi or Khoi-Khoi, who moved with herds of sheep into the coastal regions of the Cape. Later, at a date currently impossible to determine (but some time before the first European eyewitness accounts of Khoi life-style), some Khoi communities acquired cattle. They were semi-nomadic people, moving their herds from one pasture area to another, but clustered along the western and southern Cape coastal zones.

The Khoi were pastoralists, who resorted to hunting and gathering at times: they were not involved in any forms of agriculture. They lived in the south-western reaches of southern Africa, which were relatively arid, received predominantly winter rains, and had thin, sparse soils. But in the summer rainfall areas of South Africa, in the internal plateau and along the eastern seaboards, the environment and climate enabled food production through cultivation. During the first millennium, Bantu-speaking African communities were established, where domestic animals and domestic plants (mainly sorghum and millet) became the basis of people's life-style. These groups are usually referred to as farmer-pastoralists or mixed farmers. By the 6th century, such communities were well established south of the Limpopo River, and by the end of the first millennium had spread along the eastern coastal area as far south as modern East London. They were followed, during the second millennium, by Late Iron Age mixed farmers, who can be distinguished from the earlier settlements linguistically, technologically, politically and socially. From about AD 1100 onwards, the ancestors of modern Nguni-speakers – with their cattle and their crops – settled the summer rainfall areas of the east coast; and from about the 14th century the predecessors of Sotho-Tswana speakers settled Bushveld regions of the interior, before spreading further south and west across the Highveld. All of the Late Iron Age mixed-farming peoples lived in larger, more centralised, more stratified societies than those of Early Iron Age farmers. As will become evident, this had direct implications for forms of poverty.

It is sometimes assumed that before the arrival of colonial powers and settlers, there was little or no poverty in Africa: that societies were essentially egalitarian; that natural resources were abundant and freely available; and that ties of kinship and norms of reciprocity and mutuality in extended families meant that the less fortunate members of these societies were supported by others. As Selope Thema put it: 'There were no poor and rich; the haves helped those who were in want. No man starved because he had no food; no child cried for milk because its parents did not have milk cows; no orphan and old person starved … No, these things were unknown in ancient Bantu society.'[2] Sadly, this prelapsarian past never existed. Any historian of poverty in Africa is indebted to John Iliffe, and the analysis here draws directly on his pioneering work. Firstly, he makes a useful distinction between two levels of want 'that have existed in Africa for several centuries'. At the first level are very large numbers of people who are obliged to struggle continuously to preserve themselves and their dependants from physical want. The second level comprises smaller numbers who, temporarily or permanently, have failed in that struggle. Iliffe calls the first category 'the poor' and the second 'the very poor or destitute'. His book is mainly about the very poor – but also about the ways in which the ordinarily poor became very poor.[3]

Iliffe also reminds us of the distinction between conjunctural poverty and structural poverty. Conjunctural poverty is a temporary state, into which individuals or families or communities are thrust by misfortune – a natural disaster, or disease, or the like. It is a form of poverty from which, in the normal course of things, recovery is possible. Structural poverty is the long-term fate of individuals or families, due to their social circumstances beyond their control – a shortage of land, servitude, widespread unemployment, or the like. In precolonial Africa, land and natural resources were relatively abundant; and so structural poverty was the condition of those who lacked access to the labour needed to exploit land. Precolonial African society did have powerful norms of reciprocity and the protection of one's kin; but there were some who were left vulnerable. These were individuals who were too old, too young or too incapacitated to work, or who were bereft of family or other support.[4] In precolonial African communities, they were women abandoned by their husbands or widowed, orphans, the disabled. They were – as Jeff Peires remarked of the unwanted of Xhosa society – 'people who lived in Xhosaland, but were out of place there … Some were accused witches and others were disfigured – blind, albino, leprous, or just too old … All of these were peripheral to Xhosa society.'[5]

The precolonial Khoi-Khoi were a pastoral people, and as Rick Elphick points out, 'Pastoralism bred poor people ... prosperity is extremely fragile in purely pastoral societies. Families with herds of sheep or cattle could quickly become impoverished through theft, disease or drought ... the economic position of the wealthy was perpetually insecure.'[6] In consequence, many Khoikhoi clans and households experienced intermittent or conjunctural poverty. Something resembling structural poverty obtained for those with no livestock at all, such as the Strandlopers, 'the poor of Peninsular Khoikhoi society' including 'refugees, outcasts, orphans, and other persons without family'. The Strandlopers, observes Iliffe, were 'an epitome of precolonial Africa's most common categories of poor'.[7]

Moving eastwards and northwards, from the Khoi herders to the mixed farmers of the Highveld and east coast, the picture alters somewhat. Change accelerated from the mid-18th century, in the region roughly bounded by the Orange and Limpopo rivers, the Kalahari Desert and the Indian Ocean. These African societies were still independent of colonial rule, although affected by contact and interaction with traders, raiders, missionaries and travellers from colonial society. In about 1760, farming communities in this region were organised into possibly several hundred chiefdoms: small-scale units, politically decentralised, and comparatively egalitarian. But by the 1830s, the Highveld and the east coast were increasingly dominated by much larger, centralised kingdoms like the Zulu, Gaza and Ndebele, as well as smaller kingdoms like the Swazi, Basotho, Pedi, Mpondo and southern Tswana groupings. As these societies grew larger and more complex, and as political power became more centralised and overt, they also became less egalitarian, more stratified, more unequal. And this meant that they developed new patterns and forms of poverty. These kingdoms were all characterised by fairly clear divisions between three tiers: an aristocracy comprising the ruling families and their allies; secondly, a stratum of commoner families (forming the main section of the body politic) who recognised the authority of the king and looked to him for land and protection; and, thirdly, at the social base of these societies, a distinct and subordinate layer of families.[8]

It was among this lower stratum that poverty was concentrated. They tended to be people who had been captured in warfare, or the descendants of such captives. There were large numbers of people impoverished and displaced by the ravages of the *difaqane** and its aftermath, but the point being stressed here is that their emergence was a longer-term trend in these societies. They tended often not to own cattle; and frequently poor people attached themselves to cattle owners by carrying out various tasks: herding, chasing birds from

---

* The difaqane (or *mfecane*) was 'the time of troubles', the turbulent conflicts and population movements of the 1820s and 1830s.

grain fields, helping with the harvest, and performing various menial household duties. They are sometimes described as 'clients', but their status was very low, and they were often in positions of servitude similar to slavery. Among Tswana polities the poor were frequently non-Tswanas held in subjection. Among these were the Kgalagadi and a group of San people whom the Tswana called the BaSarwa. They were employed by the Tswana mainly as hunters, although children also performed domestic service in their masters' households. In the Zulu kingdom, the lowest of the three tiers consisted of members of low-status groups, at the geographic and social margins of society. They were 'despised as outsiders and inferiors by the members of the other two tiers' and given designations like *amalala* (menials), *amathonga* (servants) and *amahlengwa* (beggars).[9]

Poverty in colonial South Africa

If these were some of the faces of poverty that emerged in pre-conquest African societies, who constituted the poor in colonial societies? What were the patterns of poverty in the Dutch colony of settlement, its British successor in the 19th century, and, from the 1840s, the Boer republics across the Orange and the Vaal? One very obvious source of poverty was slavery. The Dutch East India Company (VOC) began to import slaves to its tiny colony as early as 1658; by 1692 the number of slaves in the colony exceeded that of burghers; and by the 1830s, there was a slave population of over 38,000 in the Cape. It is not just that slaves, by definition, held no property, had scant possessions, and were not earning wages; more particularly, slaves and their descendants formed a distinct layer of the poor in the Cape. Manumitted slaves and 'free blacks' were stigmatised and relegated to low-status work; but after emancipation, and the abolition of slavery, ex-slaves were extremely vulnerable. They had no savings; they had limited skills and experience; and most lacked the support provided by families or kin.

The majority of slaves worked for masters either in Cape Town itself – as general labourers, stevedores, domestic workers, masons, carpenters and so on – or in the arable western districts of Stellenbosch and Drakenstein. Here, as wheat and wine farming took hold as profitable enterprises, slave labour was crucial to their success. Slaves carried out back-breaking labour – sowing, weeding, ploughing, pruning, harvesting, threshing the grain or pressing grapes. Slave labour in the vineyards and wheat fields was integral to the formation of a Cape gentry, economically better off and relatively prosperous, making up about 10% of the settler population in the south-west. The wealthier members of this rural elite monopolised positions of authority in the *heemraden* (councils) advising the *landdrost* (magistrate) in each district; they also dominated the ranks of deacon and elder in the local church.

The existence of the gentry indicates an increasingly

stratified settler society; and, amid the lower strata, life was very different. Each of the major national groups from which immigrants arrived – Dutch, German and French – included some who were reasonably affluent, 'but many more were poverty-stricken immigrants from the lower rungs of European society'.[10] Some of the poorest signed on as VOC soldiers, out of economic desperation, entering a form of voluntary bondage for three to five years. Others found a niche in the port city as blacksmiths, tanners, tailors, cobblers, butchers and bakers; the most numerous calling among the free burghers of 18th-century Cape Town was the keeping of lodging houses.

But what about the rest of the Cape Colony, beyond the port city and the well-to-do farms? What kinds of poverty are identifiable as one considers the eastern and northerly expansion of the colony, as the trekboers fanned out into the arid and semi-arid reaches of the Karoo, the south-western coastal belt, and the plains of Camdeboo? The trekboers were stock farmers, herding sheep and cattle; there is a popular narrative that has developed about them, emphasising their self-reliance, their distance from 'civilisation', and their restless, nomadic qualities. In fact, every trekboer household required a host of items that could only be procured by trade: ironware, tools, spades, buckets, nails, string, paper, paint, turpentine, and of course gunpowder and lead. If Merrie Africa is one durable myth, there has been a parallel fable of bucolic Boer egalitarianism – according to a scholarly version, in the inland district 'class distinctions … did not apply within the white community'.[11]

But, for one thing, land was not freely available on the trekboer frontier, as suggested in older accounts. It was actually very difficult for any newcomer to find an affordable site on which to launch a career as a *veeboer* or grazier. Their best options were to work for others – as *pasgangers* or *knechten* – or to move to the very edge of the settled area.[12] The other option for landless colonists in the frontier districts was to live as a *bijwoner*, taking refuge as a tenant-by-sufferance. Their possessions were scanty and their dwellings basic. When the Cape governor Hendrik Swellengrebel toured the frontier districts in the 1770s, he reported that 'The majority here live not much better than the Hottentots … the colonists living in and nearby the principal towns are not very industrious; those living at farther distances away are even less so; they adopt fully the character of cattle herders and wild game hunters.' Susan Newton-King, on the evidence of detailed analysis of estates, has described burgher households at the lower ends of the socio-economic scale. Some were 'entirely unable to lead an independent existence'. They were typically too old to farm, or they were single men, without farms of their own. Nearly half the trekboer households in the 1760s lived in 'very straitened circumstances'.[13]

But if poorer *veeboeren* existed, and the poorest among them were entirely impoverished, a numerically much larger poor population was created in the frontier districts during the 18th century. The rate and direction of trekboer expansion were constrained for most of this century by last-ditch resistance on the part of Khoi herders and San hunters, desperate respectively to retain their livestock or their access to wild game and, in both cases, to live in the land their forebears had occupied. Fully seven decades of skirmishes, cattle raids, reprisals and intermittent conflict preceded the so-called Bushman War on the north-east frontier in the 1770s. As the Khoi lost their sheep and cattle, their social cohesion unravelled, and they lost the capacity further to resist. And so they were absorbed, as a defeated, broken people, into the economy of the frontier, as workers for the colonists. They were, says John Iliffe, 'the first numerous group in sub-Saharan Africa who were indisputably pauperised by exclusion from access to resources'.[14]

These Khoisan became farm labourers – but a distinct workforce, with its own stark characteristics. Put simply, says Newton-King, many *veeboeren* were too poor to employ free labour. Consequently, they turned to coercion to get the labour that they needed, and the Khoisan were absorbed not as wage labourers – free to sell their services, able to move from one employer to another – but in a starkly unfree relationship with their masters. Many received no wages, but were paid only in food and clothing. Labour relations on the frontier took on 'a violent, comprehensive and permanent domination more consistent with our concept of slavery than of patron-client relations'. The status of the Khoisan workers resembled in many ways that of slaves held by burghers in the south-western Cape. It is difficult to distinguish, 200 years later, between those labourers who had been war captives, those born on the farms, or those who were the issue of sexual liaisons between colonists and Khoi. What they had in common was that they were legally bound to their masters, indentured, and ruled by force. They were treated with an 'unrelenting and provocative harshness'; their treatment was justified by a set of beliefs distinguishing between Christian and heathen, citizens and non-citizens. The Khoisan remained 'forever outside the moral community' as construed by the colonists.[15] They, and their descendants, constituted a distinct stratum of the rural poor.

In the mid-19th century, another significant population of impoverished farm workers was created by war: by the violent destruction of the Xhosa kingdom in the Eastern Cape, to the west of the Kei River. The 1840s and 1850s were a pivotal moment in South African history, as English-speaking settlers in the Eastern Cape – backed by the military presence of an expansive British imperialism – destroyed Xhosa power, seized Xhosa land, and drove Xhosa men, women and children onto the labour market. The War of the Axe – or seventh frontier war – took place in 1846–7 and ended with Sir Harry Smith's theatrical and vindictive victory, and the creation of the new province of British Kaffraria. Large numbers of the amaXhosa – perhaps half of the Ngqika population – sought work in the colony, their cattle taken as war booty, their crops and homes burnt. 'Instead of entering the colony and seeking work on the free market, amaXhosa were now indentured to particular employers, at unspecified wages, even before they entered the colony.'[16]

The eighth frontier war, or Mlanjeni's War, was in many senses merely the resumption of the War of the Axe. The second-longest war ever fought in South Africa, it was waged for 27 months, from late 1850 to March 1853, with pitiless hostility by both sides; it was, concludes a recent study, 'one of the most intense and brutal colonial wars fought anywhere in the nineteenth century'. Harry Smith issued orders 'to spoil the Gaika cattle, to burn all his kraals, the fences of his corn fields, and destroy the corn fields themselves'. Colonial troops captured hundreds of thousands of cattle; approximately 16,000 Ngqika Xhosa were killed in the fighting, and many others succumbed to disease and starvation in defeat. The Ciskei's Xhosa society unravelled – and the seeds had been sown for the catastrophe of the Cattle Killing in 1856. The survivors of military defeat and slaughter of their remaining herds had no resources left. They were 'channeled off ... to the towns and farms of the

Cape Colony … herded into impromptu auctions where farmers obtained servants … [Some of] the young and orphaned … were … scattered across the entire expanse of the Cape Colony to serve long indentures labouring in the houses and farms of white settlers.' There was, writes Clifton Crais, 'a history of orphanage and abandonment here, an anthropology of anguish … that shaped the constitution of the labouring poor'.[17]

While the Cattle Killing triggered 'mass corvées of children' and orphan indentures, child labour was an important category of unfree labour long before and well after 1856. In the 18th century, settlers 'enjoyed legal title to the offspring of their slaves supplemented with children captured in raids against the indigenous population on and beyond the frontier'. The abolition of slaving increased the importance of 'compliant child labour to the … colonial economy in general and the rural settler households in particular'. Various legal mechanisms to secure indigenous, destitute, immigrant and ex-slave children were all incorporated in the Masters and Servants laws which governed the colonial labour market from 1841 onwards. The legislation created two categories of indentured child labour: destitute children, hired out by the local magistrate after advertisement in the *Government Gazette*; and those indentured by their parents, black farm workers, in exchange for livestock from their white settler employers.[18]

If the Cape Colony provided a formal, legal template

for child labour, an altogether looser, less regulated version occurred across the Vaal River. Boer colonists pressed into the interior from the late 1830s, founding towns at Potchefstroom, Lydenburg, Soutpansberg, Rustenburg and Pretoria, and in 1860 coalescing as the South African Republic (ZAR). Although the Voortrekkers considered themselves the new 'owners' of the Transvaal, their authority and control were actually very limited. They did not exercise complete dominance over African societies in the region, and a complex, shifting balance of power between Boers and African leaders persisted up to the 1880s. In these circumstances, the Voortrekkers were faced with what they perceived to be an acute shortage of labour; and they developed an impromptu but effective solution – the so-called *inboekseling* system. As soon as they arrived in the Transvaal, Boer commandos raided weaker and less organised African communities, capturing their children. These children were then 'booked in' – registered – with their new masters; *inboekseling* is usually translated as apprentice or indenture. Raids were one way that African children were transferred to Boer farmers, but they were also handed over by African societies as a form of tribute, or they were bartered and bought for cash. From the 1840s to the 1870s, there was a shift from raiding to trading as the major source of apprenticed labour. But in all cases, the *inboekseling* was housed, fed, and trained to work by his or her Boer master until the age of 21 or 25. At this point, the indenture was officially over: in practice, having known no other society since childhood, culturally and physically distanced from their societies of origin, the manumitted labourers usually stayed on as farm workers. Thus, 'between 1840 and 1870 a new underclass came into being on the Highveld of South Africa', its members unfree servants in white households and on white farms.[19]

This chapter has established that various forms of inequality and poverty existed within precolonial indigenous societies, rendering some members of their communities more vulnerable than others when it came to contacts with colonial society. The children handed over by African chiefs as *inboekseling* apprentices are a case in point. It has also considered patterns of poverty that emerged from colonial and imperial expansion in the 18th and 19th centuries. A common strand weaves its way through the patterns of settlement, farming, fighting, conquest, dispossession – and poverty. Slave labour provided the basis of colonial development in the south-west Cape; but as the trekker wagons pressed north and east, forms of coerced labour developed all along the Cape frontier, and then a distinctive form of unfree labour emerged in the Transvaal. Each of these labour regimes served the colonial economy. Each placed people of colour in subservient relations to white settlers. Each created specific forms of poverty. Subsequent chapters show that these labour regimes were succeeded by large-scale migratory labour and then by an urbanised workforce denied trade union rights or recognition. The point hardly needs belabouring. For three centuries, poverty in South Africa was profoundly shaped by changing forms of unfree labour and by social and political relations that were colour-coded.

2

The 'Poor White question' – and how it was answered

> 'It is difficult now to remember or to appreciate
> the dark shadow which poor whiteism cast
> over this country in the 1920s and 30s ... Yet
> it was the formative force in standardizing the
> relationship of black and white in this country.'
> – Margaret Ballinger

From the 18th century onwards, poverty in South Africa has been visited with particular ferocity on black people. The preceding chapter described how the first two centuries of the colonial encounter generated new categories of poverty, thrusting people of colour into various forms of coerced labour and structural dependence on their masters. Subsequent chapters reveal that as the 20th century proceeded, Africans and coloureds made up an overwhelming majority of the poor. So it might seem perverse to devote a chapter to the incidence of *white* poverty, at a particular moment in the country's history, and the steps taken first to

were others whose fortunes fell as his rose. In 1876, when Distin put up twelve miles of fencing and imported stud stallions, the civil commissioner for Middelburg reported numerous insolvencies in the district, with farmers unable to meet mortgage payments; the following year the local newspaper reported that 'most of our cultivators are in indigent circumstances'. Some of the landless whites in the district lived on Tafelberg itself – as part of Distin's labour force, housed in purpose-built servants' quarters.

The Middelburg instance was replicated elsewhere. In every district in the Karoo and Eastern Cape there was a minority of capitalising farmers, benefiting especially from the boom in wool prices. They built fences and dams; they installed pumps, windmills and other machinery; and they bought up available land with their profits. These developments meant that white squatters were forced off the land, moving usually to the nearest village or small town. There, they maintained a precarious existence, growing some of their food on an *erf* or portion of one, and earning cash through casual labour, driving carts, digging wells, selling firewood, and so on. Some of them became fully fledged wage labourers: they worked as dam-makers, fence-builders, brick-makers and quarrymen – and, once rail construction began in the Cape, as navvies along the line. In 1877, for instance, the *Eastern Province Herald* reported that many Afrikaner men sold their labour on the Midland ameliorate and, ultimately, virtually to eliminate the phenomenon. Yet a study of the 'Poor White question' and its dramatically effective solution is significant in two main respects. Firstly, it is a case study of poverty as susceptible to policy interventions. And some of those interventions, as discussed in chapter 7, provide at the very least some suggestive precedents when it comes to considering efforts to reduce poverty in South Africa today. Secondly, some of the ways in which the problem of white poverty was addressed by politicians in the early decades of the 20th century had direct, profound and lasting implications for black poverty.

The previous chapter described the existence of impoverished colonists on the Cape frontier. Men without property worked for others as *knechten* or herdsmen, or lived as *bijwoners* or squatters, their access to land by favour of those more fortunate. Others were effectively without property even while they clung to tiny and unworkable fragments of land. And from about 1860 onwards, the numbers of rural poor whites rose quite rapidly. Periods of recession dislodged many from their precarious existence; and in years of economic recovery, capitalist accumulation and agricultural improvements by well-to-do farmers could lead directly to the deepening of the poverty of their poorer neighbours. For example, J.S. Distin was the leading farmer in the Middelburg district of the Cape, who invested heavily in improving productivity on Tafelberg, his extensive farm. But there was home to the 'respectable classes'; but it was fringed by a second, 'a maze of *steegs*', lanes and alleys teeming with shacks and sheds housing the poor. 'It was the emergence of a new middle-class elite in the town that highlighted the existence of the poor', a population of freed slaves, impoverished immigrants from Britain, families displaced from the rural hinterland, and labourers who drifted in and out of employment. Although the depression of 1863 prompted some perfunctory forms of poor relief, the overall response of 'official' Cape Town was that poverty was a nuisance, but a transitory and superficial nuisance. For the British middle classes in Cape Town, the lives of the poor 'remained alien and distasteful'; the disgust shown towards District Six by Mary Maclear, wife of the Astronomer Royal, was typical: 'idle people at most of the doors and windows, or lounging about dirty and vacant'.[2]

Urban poverty was not restricted to Cape Town. Almost every town had its 'low' or 'rough' quarter where the poorest whites lived. In Port Elizabeth, fulminated a correspondent to a local newspaper, the 'district lying between Main Street and the sea' was infamous: there, black and white children grew up 'inhaling the reeking atmosphere of dung-heaps, slaughter houses and tanneries'; there 'congregated the dangerous classes, the idle and drunken'. In Grahamstown, an area known as 'bog-o'-me-finn' was 'tenanted by a miscellaneous herd of whites and blacks who lived together in the line, 'working as navvies side by side with Zulus and Fingoes', while their wives were 'engaged in a variety of menial labour'. The 1875 Cape Census helps one quantify the presence of impoverished and proletarianised whites. It detailed just under 21,000 people – out of a total adult population of 114,000 – in low-paid occupations. These included domestic servants, drivers, porters, stevedores and storemen; rail and road navvies, quarrymen, brick-makers and general labourers. The least satisfactory area of the Census was that dealing with rural occupations: the Census Report itself noted that very few of the *bijwoners* or squatters were returned as such. Yet, even so, 2,500 whites were detailed as being farm servants, agricultural labourers, herdsmen and squatters.[1]

The Census also largely omitted those whom con-temporaries styled as 'the lowest order of Europeans', 'people of the poorest sort', or 'men of the lowest class'. These were men who might once have been self-employed but were increasingly unable to support themselves. They drifted into casual employment on farms or in towns, or moved into vagrancy, begging or crime. They formed a clearly visible component of Cape society, an underclass, frequently denigrated for their idleness, licentiousness, drunkenness and other vices. In addition to the rural poverty discussed above, urban poverty was a persistent feature of the 19th-century Cape. In Cape Town itself, by the early years of the century, there were effectively two towns. In one, the neat grid of streets of the colonial port was home to the 'respectable classes'; but it was fringed by a second, 'a maze of *steegs*', lanes and alleys teeming with shacks and sheds housing the poor. 'It was the emergence of a new middle-class elite in the town that highlighted the existence of the poor', a population of freed slaves, impoverished immigrants from Britain, families displaced from the rural hinterland, and labourers who drifted in and out of employment. Although the depression of 1863 prompted some perfunctory forms of poor relief, the overall response of 'official' Cape Town was that poverty was a nuisance, but a transitory and superficial nuisance. For the British middle classes in Cape Town, the lives of the poor 'remained alien and distasteful'; the disgust shown towards District Six by Mary Maclear, wife of the Astronomer Royal, was typical: 'idle people at most of the doors and windows, or lounging about dirty and vacant'.[2]

Urban poverty was not restricted to Cape Town. Almost every town had its 'low' or 'rough' quarter where the poorest whites lived. In Port Elizabeth, fulminated a correspondent to a local newspaper, the 'district lying between Main Street and the sea' was infamous: there, black and white children grew up 'inhaling the reeking atmosphere of dung-heaps, slaughter houses and tanneries'; there 'congregated the dangerous classes, the idle and drunken'. In Grahamstown, an area known as 'bog-o'-me-finn' was 'tenanted by a miscellaneous herd of whites and blacks who lived together in the

most promiscuous manner imaginable'. In Fort Beaufort, Garrett's Lane was the site of 'a coffee shop … harbouring drunkards and idlers, black and white, from morning to night'. Clearly, an aspect of underclass poverty in the second half of the 19th century that agitated the better-off was the tendency of some of the poor of different races to live together, relax together, and sometimes work together – circumstances leading to a very real blurring of ethnic identity among the poor. The 1893 Labour Commission has a wealth of evidence about intermarriage and sexual liaisons between white and black rural and urban poor. More than once, the commissioners realised just how indistinct ethnic divisions were. In an exchange with Robert Hill, an ex-*bijwoner*, working as a post-cart driver, a commissioner asked, '[Are there] many poor whites like yourself?' and received the answer, 'I am a Coloured man. My father was a Scotchman and my mother a black woman.'[3]

Such evidence is relevant to a marked shift in ruling-class perceptions in the Cape, in the 1880s and especially the 1890s, of the nature of poverty. For much of the 20th century, it was a broadly established 'fact' that poor whites first appeared in significant numbers in the 1890s. One economic history stated firmly that there 'was virtually no absolute poverty in the country' prior to 1890; and that poor whites were created by economic forces only after the banking crisis of that year. The Carnegie Commission endorsed this chronology: it was 'especially after 1880' that 'new conditions' created a landless rural class. Thirty years ago, I questioned this orthodoxy, and did so in two main ways. First, I argued that there was a numerically substantial class of poor, proletarianised whites well before 1890; and, secondly, that what really took place in the 1890s was new ways of perceiving white poverty, of identifying it as 'the Poor White problem'.[4]

This latter argument is amplified by Vivian Bickford-Smith. He has elegantly demonstrated that before the depression of the 1880s, members of the Cape's dominant class expressed only fleeting concern about the integration of poor whites and poor blacks. But in the 1890s, a set of intersecting ideas – about the nature of poverty, about the threats to health of slum conditions, and about the dangers of 'race mixing' leading to degeneration – meant that the 'Poor White problem' was about to be discovered and defined. Politicians, churchmen, editors and other opinion-makers seized upon the 'degradation of the white population' as a crucial issue.[5] As Sarah Duff has pointed out, the racialisation of poverty discourse in the 1880s and 1890s accompanied a general shift towards a more segregated colonial society. Schools, prisons, transport, hospitals, recreation areas and workplaces all became gradually more divided along racial lines. The discovery of poor whites in the 1890s was not so much a response to any real changes in the nature of colonial poverty as it was 'a reflection of white, middle class concerns about the future of South Africa'.[6]

Gareth Stedman-Jones wrote of *fin-de-siècle* London: 'What changed in the 1890s was not so much the situation of the casual labourer as the social prism through which his situation was regarded.' In Cape Town and the rest of the colony, if one substitutes 'poor white' for 'casual labourer' the essential point is made.[7] An ideological turning point meant that white poverty had become the 'Poor White problem'. It was not so much that indigent whites were deserving as that they were dangerous, members of an underclass prone to vice and liable to slide into criminality: 'the deprived might become depraved'.[8]

If Poor White anxieties crystallised in the Cape in the 1890s, after the South African War the major location for such fears shifted north, and especially to Johannesburg. As we have seen, the process of rural proletarianisation intensified from the 1860s onwards, creating a class 'which was already in transition to lumpenproletariat status',[9] and whose members tended to move into towns and cities. Both of these features accelerated after the rinderpest epidemic of 1897 and especially after the South African War, which swept thousands of struggling Afrikaner farmers and *bijwoners* off the land for ever. In Johannesburg, for instance, the white population grew from 40,000 just before the war to nearly 250,000 by 1914. These impoverished new arrivals were poorly educated, unskilled and ill equipped for urban life. They typically moved as tenants into crowded and insanitary slums, often housing poor arrivals of many races and nationalities. Between 1907 and 1922, there was a mounting tide of concern among the city's authorities and middle classes about the existence of these slums and their residents, their threat to health, their evident miscegenation and propensity for criminality. In 1913, a government Select Committee warned that 'the European minority ... cannot allow a considerable number of its members to sink into apathetic indigency, and to fall behind the level of the non-European worker. If they do ... our race is bound to perish in South Africa.'[10] In short, urban 'poor whites became "Poor White" – a category perceived to require the state's attention'.[11]

The new Union government tackled the problem of urban slums in several ways: public health legislation, the rehousing of white workers in purpose-built housing, and the removal of black people to new, racially segregated sites. These various urban reform measures, especially in terms of segregation, were conscious attempts to contain white poverty, 'and in this sense the "poor white problem" is central to any explanation of the rise of segregation in South Africa'.[12] Official thinking about poor whites changed over time. Immediately after the South African War, white poverty was still seen as largely rural in its origins and nature, and as an expression of moral failing and hereditary weakness. But government commissions in 1913 and 1921 reframed the problem as urban in its character, and as an economic problem of ominous proportions.[13]

Politically and ideologically, white poverty served as a lightning rod; it 'concentrated and discharged anxieties'.[14] Such anxieties were acute. As E.G. Malherbe, who initiated the Carnegie Commission inquiry into white poverty, recalled years later, poor whites were 'a menace to the self-preservation and prestige of the white people'.[15] Many poor whites were Afrikaners, and this was a source of particular alarm to ministers of the Dutch Reformed Church and to Afrikaner nationalist politicians, who were among the first to call for action. White poverty moved to the political centre stage with the formation in 1924 of the Pact government, a coalition between Hertzog's National Party and the Labour Party, with Hertzog as Prime Minister. The Pact government was doubly sensitive to the issue of white poverty: on the one hand, most of the poor whites were Afrikaners; on the other hand, the Labour Party was pledged to reduce white unemployment levels. The Pact government appointed the Carnegie Commission, which delivered its massive report on the 'Poor White question' in 1933 – which Grace Davie judges 'arguably the most important study of poverty in South African history'.[16]

The Pact government and its successor, the Fusion government headed by Hertzog, sought to reduce white poverty through three main approaches. Firstly, a legislative package regulated the labour market to protect white workers from competition. The 'civilised labour policy' relied partly on a job colour bar, creating a rigid caste arrangement between white and black workers to the benefit of the former; and partly on improved wages for white workers. Whites should be guaranteed wages that enabled them to live at 'civilised' – i.e. white – standards of living. The Industrial Conciliation Act of 1924, the Wage Act of 1925 and the Mines and Works Amendment Act (accurately nicknamed the Colour Bar Act) of 1926 had a considerable combined effect. They created a system of industrial relations, but with a definition of employee that effectively excluded all African workers from its operations; they enabled a Wage Board to set minimum wages for white workers not incorporated in the industrial councils; and they ensured that certain skilled occupations became the sole preserve of white workers. Unskilled white workers were protected by minimum wage levels; skilled white workers won rights to monopolise the best-paid niches of employment.[17]

The second element was an ambitious programme of public works, to create jobs for whites. By 1933, about 59,000 poor whites were employed in various relief measures – irrigation schemes, road and dam building, and rail construction. State spending on these relief measures rose exponentially: from 2.6% of the budget in 1930 to 15.8% by 1933. In terms of job creation, unskilled and semi-skilled white workers were employed on the railways, which replaced black workers with white, and in the new state-owned iron and steel giant, ISCOR. Between 1924 and 1933, unskilled white workers rose from 9.5% of the workforce on the railways to 39.3%. By 1939, the central government employed 98,000 white workers, over half of whom were on relief works. In the short term, it was the 'introduction of a systematic and elaborate Public Works Programme' that most rapidly eliminated white poverty.[18]

The third thrust of Pact and Fusion policies saw the sustained expansion of government services to white families, especially education, health and housing. In the 1930s, the central government made available funds that enabled Johannesburg to provide subsidised public housing for white families. The Slums Act was implemented by the city council so as to achieve 'removing all slum dwellers and re-housing only the whites'.[19] There was a massive drive to improve the standards of white schooling, a 'state-supported diffusion of numeracy, literacy and skills' for white children. It was this investment in human capital that in the longer term eliminated white poverty. Linked to the provision of public services to white families was a massive increase of social welfare provisions, funded by the state, with primarily white beneficiaries.

In 1928, the Pact government passed an Old Age Pensions Act. In a distinctively South African irony, this progressive initiative was racially motivated, an explicit response to fears of *swartgevaar* and anxieties about white poverty. 'In this country', said a National Party MP, 'there is a small number of whites against the natives, a few civilised people against uncivilised hordes, and for that reason it is so important that not a single white person should be allowed to go under.'[20] The Act made pensions available to white and coloured men and women. They were non-contributory, funded entirely by the state: unusual anywhere at the time and exceptional in the global South. Pensions were means-tested, and they were racially skewed. Whites received £30 p.a. and coloureds £18. Africans and Indians were excluded – the former on the grounds that 'native custom ... makes provision for maintaining dependent persons'.[21] In the 1930s, other forms of state-funded social protection were added: unemployment benefits, job programmes, pensions for the blind, disability grants, welfare for poor children. These went mainly to white beneficiaries and, to a lesser extent, to coloureds. In 1937, a separate Department of Social Welfare was created; a year later almost £10 million, or 20% of public expenditure, was spent on social welfare services. By 1939, writes Jeremy Seekings, South Africa had 'created the basis of a remarkable welfare state', although a highly racialised one. Whites, and to a lesser extent coloureds, were the beneficiaries; Indians and Africans were almost entirely excluded.[22]

In short: policies of the Pact and Fusion governments protected white workers against competition from black workers, and created jobs for unemployed whites. They also ensured that white families would receive the best education, best social care, best job opportunities and highest pensions. These policies, and the rapid recovery from the Depression from 1933 onwards, meant that white poverty declined sharply. By 1936, the Department of Labour and Social Welfare announced that there was no longer a surplus of white labour. Full employment for whites had been effectively achieved. By 1942, white poverty was to all practical purposes eliminated.

But the 'solution' of the 'Poor White question' had profound and lasting implications for black poverty. African mine workers were frozen out of skilled work 'not because they lacked the competence to do it, but ... precisely because they were, or soon would be, competent'. Other African workers were excluded from the apprenticeship system; rendered ineligible for membership in recognised trade unions; and locked into a low wage regime, deliberately maintained by state policy. In the inter-war years, reducing white poverty became a political priority; in addressing it 'the state increasingly defined the relationship between white prosperity and white supremacy'. Replicating 'civilised' standards of living for the white minority – remark Nattrass and Seekings – could be sustained 'only through systematic discrimination against the majority'.[23]

3

Poor blacks
Rural and urban
poverty before 1948

*'The farm labourer in my experience is badly
nourished. I have a recollection of a number of
post-mortem examinations which I performed
on Natives on farms and they had hardly any
superficial fat and their bowels were very thin
… It seems to me that a Native ages a great deal
earlier than he should. A Native in his fifties is
pretty well worn out.'*
– District Surgeon for Aliwal North, to Natives
Economic Commission, 1932

If white poverty was so successfully addressed, what
about black poverty in the first half of the 20th century?
In policy terms, the distinction could hardly have been
starker. Policy-makers were aware of both rural and
urban poverty among the African population, but did
little to address the symptoms, let alone the causes of
such poverty. At the risk of oversimplifying, one can iden-

tify three key responses to black poverty: segregation, parsimony and social control. Segregation proceeded, firstly, from the premise that Africans properly belonged in 'native reserves', as demarcated by the 1913 Land Act (and extended in 1936); secondly, that towns and cities were European domains, where black people should only enter 'to minister to the needs of whites' and should depart from there when they 'ceased so to minister'; and, thirdly, that while black people were busy ministering to white needs, they should be confined to particular areas of the city. Black poverty was to be kept spatially separate, both in the countryside and in cities and towns. Rural dwellers were outsiders in relation to city-dwellers; but black urbanites were outsiders in relation to whites. This dual exclusion was fundamental to South Africa's social geography of extremes.

Parsimony was embedded in the reluctance by white voters and politicians to pay for black welfare or progress. It also involved ingenious methods to ensure that Africans, however poor, bore the main costs of their administration. In urban areas, the template was the 'Durban system', which involved the creation of a municipal beer monopoly: African men could drink sorghum beer only at special municipal beer halls. The revenue from beer sales was then earmarked for municipal expenditure on Africans – for example, the construction of municipal barracks or hostels, and a police force directly financed by beer revenue.[1] The 'Durban system' was then made national, in the 1923 Natives Urban Areas Act. It allowed for the establishment of municipal beer monopolies in every city; and separated the financing of the locations from that of the city by creating a separate, self-balancing native revenue account. The same logic was applied in the 'native reserves': locally collected hut-tax, quitrents and other fees were used to pay for the highly limited infrastructure and services in these areas.

The third generic policy response towards black poverty was to strengthen social control over the black population, to tighten the grip of white supremacy. Long before apartheid was launched in 1948, the South African state 'developed an extensive apparatus of repression based primarily on control over movement'. Passes and permits 'allowed the ruling classes to keep African workers in a permanent state of subordination'.[2] Stringent measures controlled where Africans lived, worked, were schooled – and on what terms. In towns and cities, administering and policing black inhabitants was placed largely in the hands of local authorities by the 1923 Urban Areas Act. From the 1930s, as government reluctantly accepted that African urbanisation was inevitable, the central state nibbled away at local powers – a dynamic accelerated after 1948. In the reserves, the Native Affairs Department in effect delegated local control to chiefs and headmen, and in the inter-war years 'intervened more systematically to appoint cooperative men'.[3]

Rural poverty

There is no watertight line between rural and urban poverty. African families had members who experienced both rural and urban poverty; and migrant labour impelled men from rural poverty to work in low-waged urban poverty. But rural and urban forms of poverty can be analysed separately. This chapter commences in the countryside: it is important to remember that in the first half of the 20th century South Africa was demographically a predominantly rural society. In 1948, three-quarters of the total African population remained rooted in rural areas – 39% in the reserves and 35% on white-owned land. About 26% of Africans in 1948 lived in towns and cities.[4]

In 1925, the historian W.M. Macmillan was asked by the government's Department of Statistics to make a detailed investigation of a single district, Herschel, which was almost entirely demarcated as a reserve. Almost 40,000 Africans lived in 680 square miles, an area easily distinguishable from its white neighbours because it had 'obviously received no tangible or visible benefit from public expenditure on its needs', lacking roads, bridges, public buildings. Macmillan's carefully collated data indicated that in a good year the district could provide half its food requirements; that over 11,000 men left the district each year to earn the wages needed to survive, working on farms and in mines, i.e. 75% of the adult males left home each year; that there was a growing minority of adult men who had 'no land to till and little prospect of acquiring land'; and, in his sombre conclusion, 'A huge proportion of the community here depicted exists almost on the very lowest level of bare subsistence.'[5]

Macmillan also wrote about the reserves more broadly. Central to his analysis of poverty in the reserves was the history of dispossession: 'the Bantu millions have had to face a prodigious social revolution. They have been called upon, in the space of three generations or less, to adapt themselves, somehow or other, to live on what may be put at a rough estimate at about one-fifth of the land they lately held.' Africans in the reserves were 'immeasurably poorer' than they had been; they lived in 'poverty, congestion and chaos', blighted by 'ill-health, and starvation, endemic typhus, and almost chronic scurvy'; they suffered 'an often appalling mortality rate among infants'; they lived in 'heavily over-populated' and 'grossly neglected' areas where they were 'utterly dependent on wage-earning outside' to relieve 'a dead level of poverty' inside.[6]

Macmillan was writing over 80 years ago. Yet his characterisation of poverty in the reserves 'remained unrivalled within the corpus of South African studies for almost half a century'; his insights into agrarian change 'retained such freshness and trenchancy fifty years later' that they fed directly into the radical historiography of the 1970s.[7] Recent scholarship has refined and nuanced

Macmillan's findings, while broadly confirming them. A sophisticated overview of agricultural production in the reserves shows that from 1918 until 1955 the total agricultural product in these areas was more or less static, producing on average just under half of food requirements. Charles Simkins calls this a period of 'fragile productivity maintenance', followed by a 'period of rapid decline'. After 1955 this proportion fell rapidly, to 26% by 1963. In parts of the Transkei, especially the eastern coastal areas, and in Zululand, families could produce a higher proportion of their subsistence needs for longer than other reserves. The northern Cape, Transvaal and Orange Free State reserves occupied an intermediate position; the Ciskei and the reserves in Natal were the worst off. Taking the reserves as a whole, 'one finds that their inhabitants were far from able to provide for their subsistence requirements from agricultural production as early as 1918'.[8]

More recently, Charles Feinstein, author of incomparably the best recent economic history of South Africa, assesses reserve conditions in similar terms. By the 1920s, he writes, 'Even the largest, potentially fertile areas [in the reserves] were under extreme pressure, with the population increasing and the condition of the land deteriorating.' He quotes a survey of conditions in the Ciskei in the 1940s which 'concluded grimly that without the earnings of the emigrants, the population of the district would starve ... even with migrant remittances, the toll of death and disease was exceedingly high.' The 'tragedy of the reserves', their 'desperate conditions and continuous deterioration', ensured a supply of labour for the mines and for white farms.[9] Africans in the reserves had to sell their labour power in order to survive; but their poverty drastically lessened their bargaining power. The reserves had become 'a world where labour was almost the only defence against poverty'.[10] Extreme poverty (except when famine struck – about half a dozen times between 1910 and 1950, in different parts of the country)[11] was staved off for the majority of those living in the reserves between the wars by the remittances of migrant workers. Those who experienced extreme poverty were people unable to work and without employed family members.

The structural poverty of the reserves has easily identifiable components: population growth exerting pressure on a finite amount of land; overstocking and overgrazing causing erosion and declining fertility; very few employment opportunities within the reserves; a workforce of poorly educated and low-skilled men; and a constant pattern of indebtedness to local traders. But, as already indicated, it is impossible to comprehend reserve poverty without reference to the institution of large-scale migrant labour. By 1910, there were already 200,000 men working in the gold mines; migrant labour had become an essential part of the economy of all the African reserves, and of most households within them.

By 1920, the Chamber of Mines ran a highly centralised recruiting system, drawing men from the Eastern Cape, Natal and Transvaal reserves, as well as from Lesotho, Mozambique and Nyasaland. Miners were hired on fixed-term contracts and housed in huge, single-sex compounds. The Native Labour Regulation Act of 1911 made breach of contract a criminal offence, and taking part in a strike illegal. This combination of fixed-term contracts, compound life and penal sanctions meant that the Chamber of Mines developed 'modern, quasi-totalitarian instruments of control' over its workers, in 'one of the world's most regimented labour systems'[12] – and this labour system was historically sustainable *because* of poverty in the reserves.

Such control translated into the mining industry's ability to keep African miners' wages artificially low. Between 1911 and 1961, wages in real terms actually fell by 14%. The mining industry constantly justified the level of wages with the argument that the needs of the families of mine workers were met by the income from farming. By the 1940s, it was almost impossible to be unaware of the dearth in the reserves. The National Nutritional Council reported in 1944 that 'The pellagra … group of diseases is on the increase … There are also more general signs of the lack of food. The thin, round-shouldered, flat-chested, pot-bellied child with spindly legs was such a common sight that it could only be concluded that many were on the borders of starvation.'

Death rates in the reserve areas had been 40% higher in 1936 than in 1921: 'practically all diseases prevalent in the Native reserves are associated with malnutrition and personal poverty'. Almost impossible not to know – yet listen to the Chamber of Mines in its evidence to the Mine Wages Committee in 1943. It extolled the 'attractive and healthy individual existence of the Native and his family in the reserves'; it explained that 'the Native's independent position as peasant farmer and stock holder' assured him of 'his prolonged holiday at home'. Was there, the Chamber demanded, 'any other body of workers in the world so fortunately placed?'[13]

The 1951 Census found that 3.3 million Africans lived in the reserves; a further 2.6 million lived and worked on white-owned land. Families living on white farms comprised four main categories: cash tenancy, sharecropping, labour tenancy and wage labour. Cash tenants were mainly on farms owned by land companies or by absentee landlords. Sharecroppers paid their landlords in kind, with a share of what they produced. Labour tenants farmed a portion of a white-owned farm and paid rent in the form of a specified amount of labour, typically 60 or 90 days a year. In 1910, only a small minority of Africans on white-owned land were full-time wage earners. Over the next five decades, there was a gradual, uneven but inexorable shift in these relations, away from the more independent forms of tenancy towards labour tenancy and wage labour. As farming became more commercial and more profitable, employers wanted a more tightly controlled and readily available workforce. Labour tenancy remained the dominant form of tenure in the inter-war years, in Natal, the Free State and the Transvaal; but the terms of tenancy became increasingly harsh and demanding. Farmers wanted more family members to work for more days each year, and sought to whittle away the ability of Africans to produce their own crops and run their own herds.

In the years after Union, 'new modes of mobilising, organising, utilising and disciplining [farm] labour emerged'.[14] By the mid-1920s, farmers were served by nearly 300 labour recruiters who specialised in channelling workers onto white farms. Farmers, as the mining companies had done before, relied partly on foreign migrant labour: large maize and potato farmers were buying '12 month boys' from outside the country.[15] Like the mines before them, farmers housed their contracted migrant labourers in purpose-built closed compounds. Like migrant miners, migrant farm workers were subject to constant surveillance and relentless discipline. Compounds were fenced off, guarded, and locked at night to prevent desertion. The working day was rigidly regimented, with overseers relying on the whip for discipline; on many farms, workers' clothes were confiscated during working hours – again, to prevent desertion – and back-breaking labour was carried out wearing mealie-sacks. Food rations consisted largely of mealie-meal; illness and malnutrition were rife. Often, those signed on as migrants were precisely workers who were 'too ill, too malnourished or incapacitated to find work elsewhere'.[16]

Unsurprisingly, farm work was the least attractive form of employment in South Africa. Farmers who wanted more hands at work on their farms could hardly rely upon the free play of the labour market – and so they relied on legislation to protect and regulate the supply of labour at very low wages. In 1932, the Native Service Contract Act was passed, a law of 'unsurpassed repressive qualities'. It eroded the relative independence of labour tenant families by allowing farmers to evict the whole family if a single member failed to render service; gave African parents the power to enter binding contracts on behalf of their children; and introduced whipping for contraventions of Masters and Servants laws.[17] In addition to the wide-scale use of migrant contracts, two other forms of cheap farm labour are worth noting. First, the use of child labour was integral to the rural economy, not just in the first half of the 20th century but much later. It is estimated that there were over 60,000 black child farm labourers in 1990.[18] Secondly, white farmers also received state assistance in securing a workforce through the use of prison labour. The first large-scale scheme using convicts as farm workers was introduced between 1929 and 1931, 'without legal sanction, Parliamentary blessing, or any semblance of legitimacy'.[19] The Prisons Department 'sold off' short-term black prisoners to maize farmers. In 1947, two steps were taken that marked a massive increase in prison labour. One was the construction of purpose-built farm jails, paid for by local farmers, and run by the Department of Prisons. The other was a scheme whereby petty offenders could choose to work as farm labour rather than face imprisonment.[20] The use of prison labour on farms reached its apex in the 1950s, before a series of exposés discredited the practice.

This section has described two main forms of rural poverty. In the African reserves, poverty was a function of over-population and declining productivity, expressed as a subsistence crisis that made very high levels of male migrant labour an inescapable economic necessity. On white-owned farms, poverty was a function of a black resident farm-worker class occupying the lowest rungs of the labour market, marginalised and super-exploitable. Its members were tied by pass laws to the land and by Masters and Servants laws to their employers; over the decades, their ability to produce food and income for themselves was hacked away, their wages kept abysmally low.

Urban poverty

Periods of rapid urbanisation, wherever they take place, have historically tended to create forms of urban poverty: for the 19th century, think of the teeming slums of London's East End as described by Chadwick, or

Manchester as described by Engels; of tenements in New York and Chicago described by Jacob Riis and Upton Sinclair. South Africa was no exception to this pattern. The rapid growth of cities after the mineral discoveries and the construction of rail lines led to a similar, rapid proliferation of urban slums.[21] Poverty in inner-city slums was initially multiracial; in the 1920s and 1930s strenuous efforts were made to remove poor white people from these settings, and white urban poverty largely disappeared. This left distinctive and successive forms of black urban poverty: inner-city slumyards; shantytowns; squatter settlements; the construction of segregated townships with basic residences and minimal facilities; and subletting and rack-renting in 'locations' or townships. Each South African city manifested poverty in its own distinctive way, but one can also identify some general features of urban poverty up to the 1950s.

Firstly, acute poverty was never as widespread in cities during these years as it was in the countryside. Individuals or families could of course be thrust into destitution – by the illness, death or desertion of the main wage earner or, as in the 1930s, when the Depression saw employers lay off workers – but most city-dwellers, most of the time, escaped extreme poverty. Urbanised families usually had one or more members earning wages, in domestic service or in slightly better-paying jobs in the formal sector. Their poverty was the structural outcome of persistently low wages paid to African workers.

Africans in the cities were poor even when they were employed – but they were not as poor as their rural cousins. A careful study by economists estimated that in 1936 the per capita income of urbanised Africans was £31 per year, compared with figures of £7 for Africans on white farms and £3 for those living in the reserves.[22]

Secondly, as black families settled in South African cities, they adapted to and experimented with new forms – *urban* forms – of housing, work and leisure; lived in new urban communities; and experienced the opportunities and frustrations of city life. And so there emerged new and distinctive forms of urban culture and identities among African city-dwellers. One cultural form was that of *marabi*, which emerged on the Witwatersrand, in the network of slumyards that proliferated through western, eastern and central parts of the city in the decades before segregation was fully imposed. At the heart of *marabi* culture was the shebeen, with the consumption of alcohol, with a syncretic style of music, with clothing as modern and modish as could be afforded, with relations between men and women released from the constraints of customary belief. 'But marabi meant more. It meant youth and modernity. It meant the freedom of the town. It meant the freedom of towns not yet in the grip of the state. It meant hope and ambition not yet crushed.'[23]

The best known instance of urban culture emerged in Sophiatown. By the 1940s it was 'glamorous if seedy … a uniquely innovative, interactive place, twanging with short-term optimism and creative energy'. Sophiatown was 'materially poor but intensely social; crime-ridden and violent but neighbourly and self-protective; proud, bursting with music and writing, swaggering with personality, simmering with intellectual and political militance. [It was] a slum of dreams, a battleground of the heart.'[24] In East London's East Bank township too, in the 1940s and 1950s, a 'new cosmopolitan style' combined sport, music, fashion, entertainment and politics in a distinctively urban blend. The location youth at the time 'were imprinted with a powerful sense that they were part of something new, something very modern'; there was an 'explosion of new music groups, sports clubs and dancing styles'. A former resident recalled nostalgically that 'it felt like we had become the Sophiatown of the Eastern Cape'.[25]

Thirdly, the pattern, pace and politics of African urbanisation were central to black aspirations and white anxieties throughout the 20th century. For seven decades after Union, successive governments tried to restrict, retard and even reverse the movement into towns by African families. From Colonel Stallard to H.F. Verwoerd, segregation and apartheid were variants of a 'politics of population ... preoccupied with trying to reconfigure spatial ratios of blacks to whites and regulate the conditions of their association'.[26] Mine owners and many politicians favoured single migrant labourers rather than settled wage earners with families;

government used the paraphernalia of the Urban Areas Act to restrict African access to the cities. And once municipalities and governments were confronted with the fact of permanent black residents, they moved to segregate them, displacing them from the city proper to drab, uniform, purpose-built dormitory townships. Townships were located at a distance from the city centre and white suburbs; they were designed to facilitate policing and control, a distinctive chapter in the 'politics of population'. As Dr W.M. Eiselen, Secretary for Native Affairs, explained in 1951, 'Only by provision of adequate shelter in properly planned native townships can full control over urban natives be regained.'[27]

How were these broad features expressed in different South African cities? Johannesburg dominates any account of urbanisation in South Africa, by virtue of its sheer size, mushroom growth, variety of experiences, and intensity of urban struggles at various times. As early as 1904, Johannesburg's African population was recorded as over 55,000; successive census totals subsequently show rapid growth: 1921 – 118,353; 1936 – 229,122; 1946 – 387,175; 1951 – 465,266.[28] By 1921, Africans in Johannesburg lived in four main residential types: migrant compounds on the gold mines; purpose-built municipal 'locations' beginning with Klipspruit in 1905 and Western Native Township in 1918; rented property in slumyards; and freehold property in Alexandra and Sophiatown. To these would be added, in the 1940s, shantytowns built by squatters' movements. By the mid-1920s, just over 50,000 African men were housed in mining compounds; only 17,000 Africans lived in township housing; and an estimated 40,000 rented quarters in the inner-city slumyards of Doornfontein, Fordsburg, Ferreirastown, Marshalltown and Vrededorp. These were classic inner-city slums: densely occupied by tenants who paid negligent and uncaring landlords for their grimy quarters. In the early years of the 20th century, this inner-city area was a zone of mixed-race slums. 'As such areas became poorer, the skins of their inhabitants tended to become darker', a pervasive phenomenon in South African urban history.[29]

Such slumyards were a source of great anxiety to the city council, and over the 1930s and 1940s they were largely demolished. A remarkable piece of research carried out in the early 1930s, by Ellen Hellman, bequeathed a vivid picture of life in one slumyard, which she called Rooiyard.[30] The yard was in Doornfontein, less than two kilometres from the city centre, owned by a white landlord. Its 107 rooms housed 376 people, as well as a shifting population of visiting relatives and friends. Hellman reveals what these people earned, what they ate, how they relaxed; she reveals that women were constantly 'washing, scrubbing, polishing and dusting' – and that the rooms held furniture, bicycles, sewing machines and the like, usually bought on hire purchase. Most men's wages did not cover monthly expenditure, and were supplemented by income from women or casual work by children. One in five Rooiyard women worked as domestic servants or washerwomen; a larger number supplemented family income by brewing and selling beer. 'While older people clung to rural values, the young adopted the marabi style and pursued money and advancement with cheerful ruthlessness.'[31]

Densely tenanted yards also existed in the two freehold African townships of Alexandra and Sophiatown. Alexandra combined the 'notoriety of the crime-ridden slum with the renown of the resilient and resistant community'. Yards were a square space holding one major house – often granted to a better-off elite soon after the township was founded in 1912 – but over the decades filled also with smaller, often single-roomed, dwellings. Extensive subletting by the standholder was the order of the day, creating a densely packed community with a strong sense of belonging. The yard system also meant that a small elite of teachers, town councillors, policemen, doctors and nurses 'lived side by side, in the same yard ... with the unemployed, domestic servants, factory workers and beggars'.[32] A single room in Alex – 'a shack, with a dirt floor, no heat, no electricity, no running water' – built by the standholder Mr Xhoma was the first place Nelson Mandela regarded as home. While he remembered the crime, over-crowding and poverty of the township, he also recalled it as 'a kind of heaven'; a community with a sense of solidarity, where poverty was leavened by generosity.[33]

By way of contrast, East London was a very different urban setting. The least industrialised South African city in the first half of the 20th century, its city council actively discouraged any permanent urban settlement by Africans. This meant that a higher proportion of Africans in the city retained 'intimate and persistent' relations with their rural homes; in the mid-1930s, it was estimated that only 30% of the city's Africans were fully urbanised. Deterioration of the Ciskeian reserves had seen the city's African population reach over 30,000 people, and by 1950 fully 50,000. Wage levels were lower than in other cities, and the new arrivals lived in conditions of deprivation and insecurity. The largest location, on the East Bank of the Buffalo River, was one of the most over-crowded in South Africa, 'a festering, uncontrolled slum with open sewers'. In 1929, the Medical Officer of Health reported an infant mortality rate that had reached the 'appalling' rate of 543 deaths per 1000 births. For the decade as a whole, it averaged over 333 per 1000.[34] East London was arguably home to the most acute urban poverty in South Africa between 1910 and 1948.

Durban had its own distinctive pattern of urbanisation. From early in the 20th century, city authorities strove to ensure that Africans in the city should be as impermanent and as migratory as possible; and, to this end, used the beer-hall revenue to build single-sex male hostels. But the hostels never housed more than a third of the city's African population. By the 1930s, poverty in the Natal reserves and evictions of labour tenants from farms saw Africans pour into Durban: the estimated African population swelled from 44,000 in 1932 to 150,000 by 1949. The newcomers were variously housed: in domestic servants' quarters, in private barracks, as tenants in white-owned backyards, and increasingly in shacks on land owned by Indians. By 1950, perhaps 50,000 Africans lived in the Cato Manor shantytown. Cato Manor typified an inter-war form of African urbanisation: a shack settlement whose inhabitants were poor but 'created for themselves new economic, social and political spaces'. In Cato Manor, Africans became sub-landlords, traders, hawkers, painters, mechanics and shack-builders: it was precisely this sort of autonomy and independence that made such settlements particularly objectionable to apartheid planners, as discussed in chapter 4.[35]

Finally, Cape Town's urban poverty had its own local characteristics. Demographically, Cape Town was distinctive for having a smaller proportion of Africans in its population; and in having far larger numbers of people classified as coloured among the poor and destitute. When Professor Edward Batson published his pioneering social survey of poverty in Cape Town in 1941, he reported that 53% of the city's non-white households – predominantly coloured – were living below the poverty datum line (compared with 5% of white families). By the late 1930s, another feature of poverty in Cape Town was gathering pace: the establishment of 'uncontrolled peri-urban squatting on the Cape Flats, in Windermere and in Retreat'. The poor families in these squatter camps were both African and coloured. During World War II, new cohorts of Africans migrated to the city from the Eastern Cape. Many were unemployed, adding to 'the already swollen ranks of the poor'. They also increased the squatter population on the Cape Flats, prone to flooding in winter. By the early 1940s, the shantytowns of Windermere, Epping Forest and Blouvlei were home to over 50,000 people, whose living conditions were so scandalous that they were debated in parliament.[36]

This chapter has argued, firstly, that South Africa's cities displayed many of the characteristics typical of rapid urbanisation anywhere, notably the creation of slum conditions housing new arrivals and poorer members of the population. Secondly, the primary response of the authorities to such slums was segregation, creating distinctive racial and spatial patterns of poverty. Thirdly, every South African city urbanised in its own way, with its own distinctive features in the handling of black poverty. But they shared a desire to slow the growth of black city-dwellers; and to control as tightly as possible the lives of those black people who did live there. By the 1940s, urban authorities had failed to achieve either of these goals. This failure was central to the outcome of the 1948 general election, and to the policies of apartheid.

Apartheid and urban poverty

'I was very small, you see, when my mother and my father they threw me away. There was no more money. And so okay while the years and months passed by, you see, I found myself in a stony place of sadness and madness where each dog was hustling for his own bone.'

– Aapie, interviewed in Cape Town
by Don Pinnock

Apartheid proper lasted just over 40 years, from 1948 to 1990. The next four years were transitional, an apartheid twilight or democratic dawn. But four decades is a long time for a political project to run; 40 years of apartheid 'gave South African society a distinctive profile and a long shadow'[1] – and during these years there were major developments in the history of South African poverty. Some forms of poverty were the direct result of apartheid policies; some were the consequence of neglect or indifference; others arose almost independently of policy, as part of the broader economic history of these years. Understanding the history of poverty during apartheid is essential when it comes to addressing the challenges of poverty and inequality in South Africa today. It helps reveal how many people were poor in the mid-1990s, how poor they were, why they were poor, and how poverty affected their lives.

This chapter briefly identifies the major features of apartheid and its successive phases, before considering changing patterns of poverty in the cities. As chapter 3 made plain, South Africa was already a highly segregated society prior to apartheid. Political power was in white hands; the lives of the black majority were tightly controlled and regulated. There was also a taken-for-granted segregation of institutions and everyday social life. Apartheid made segregation more systematic and discrimination more absolute; it created 'a monstrously labyrinthine system which dominated every facet of life';[2] and its machinery of repression and control required ever more authoritarian means to maintain it. So far, so familiar. But apartheid was not a single, seamless project, driven by a grand plan. Devising and implementing apartheid included its share of uncertainties, compromises and retreats. In broad terms, there were three main phases of apartheid: 1948 to 1960; 1960 to 1974/5; and the mid-1970s to the early 1990s.

The implementation of apartheid, 1948–60
The term 'apartheid' only entered political life in the 1940s, as a call for more rigorous racial separation,

but with no specifics. The slogan provided a general direction of travel and not a route map. The first period of apartheid saw a number of new policies written into the statute book, grouped here in five broad categories:

- There was a greater emphasis on racial identities and racial boundaries. The Population Registration Act required every South African to be registered as belonging to one of four races. As the Minister of the Interior, Dönges, pointed out, 'The determination of a person's race is of the greatest importance in the enforcement of any existing or future laws.' The Prohibition of Mixed Marriages Act and the Immorality Act addressed anxieties about racial mixing; the Group Areas Act ensured that cities and towns would be zoned on racial lines.

- Apartheid legislation extended control by the central state over education and housing. H.F. Verwoerd, Minister of Native Affairs from 1950, was more ideologically confident and ambitious than any other NP politician. He introduced the Bantu Education Act in terms that could not have been plainer: 'The Bantu must be guided to serve his own community … There is no place for him in the European community above the level of certain forms of labour.' The Natives Resettlement Act gave government sweeping powers to rehouse Africans living in racially mixed areas.

- New powers sought to control urban influx even more rigorously, to keep the settled urban African population as small as possible, without jeopardising the economy. The core intention was to restrict the numbers of fully urbanised Africans, and it was reflected in the notorious 'Section 10' rights. Africans could qualify for urban 'residential rights' only if they had been born and lived continuously in a particular city, or had worked for a single employer for the previous ten years. Anyone not meeting these criteria was not entitled to remain in a city for more than 72 hours.

- The white monopoly of political power was further buttressed. Coloured voters in the Cape were removed from the voters' roll, and Africans totally excluded from central political institutions. In return, they were provided with an elaborate system of limited local government in the reserves, which strengthened the powers of chiefs and 'traditional' leaders.

- Finally, the 1950s inflated the coercive powers of the state and reduced existing civil rights. A barrage of laws outlawed various forms of political protest; and in 1956, determined to extinguish black defiance, the government arrested ANC leaders, trade unionists and activists and charged them with high treason.

Thus, the first phase of apartheid entrenched and extended segregation; imposed sweeping bureaucratic controls over black people; centralised and strengthened state power; and criminalised most black political opposition. However, this phase failed in one of its basic objectives: to contain, or slow down, the movement of Africans to urban areas. The black urban population rose by nearly 50% between 1950 and 1960, from 2.6 million to 3.8 million people; and there was no end in sight to political protests mounted by predominantly urban political organisations. These were the immediate triggers to the second phase of apartheid.

The high tide of apartheid, 1960–74

These years saw apartheid's apogee, the project at its peak. Apartheid took on new dimensions as Verwoerd's government inaugurated an ideological and strategic shift.[3] As the National Party (NP) shifted to a more aggressive and authoritarian phase of policy-making, its support from white South Africans markedly increased. In the late 1960s and early 1970s, the apartheid regime won more votes from white South Africans than before or afterwards. In 1966, Verwoerd won an electoral landslide, the NP sweeping 126 of 166 seats.

Beyond the tepid waters of white parliamentary politics, the government's dominance was even more pronounced. After Sharpeville, and the bannings of the ANC and PAC, both organisations set up underground structures and launched violent forms of struggle. Verwoerd and Minister of Justice B.J. Vorster responded with legislation providing for detention without trial, solitary confinement and swingeing penalties for sabotage and terrorism (offences almost laughably broadly defined). The Rivonia Trial saw Mandela and other ANC leaders jailed for life. Thousands of rank-and-file members of the ANC and PAC were arrested, tried, and imprisoned. By the mid-1960s, organised African opposition inside the country had been effectively extinguished.

Economically, these were boom years. Between 1960 and 1970, GDP grew at over 5% a year. Middle-class whites enjoyed an unprecedented affluence. Foreign investors recovered their nerve after Sharpeville, grateful that political authority had been asserted and prepared to ignore the terms on which this had been done. In 1970, the *Wall Street Journal* reported that for 260 American companies with significant foreign investments, South Africa provided the highest returns. Two years later, the investors' magazine *Fortune* noted drily that 'South Africa has always been regarded by foreign investors as a gold mine, one of those rare and refreshing places where profits are great and problems small. Capital is not threatened by political instability or nationalisation. Labor is cheap, the market booming, the currency hard and convertible.'[4]

This was the context of apartheid's second phase, often called 'grand apartheid'. Its two key features were a vision of self-governing ethnic statelets, and a ruthlessly ambitious programme of social engineering. The 'grand apartheid' policy was first announced in 1959, when Verwoerd told parliament that in due course blacks would be led to 'full development' and 'full authority' in 'their own areas'. The apartheid regime would guide African ethnic 'nations' to 'govern properly and to assume responsibility' in their 'homelands'. How 'grand apartheid' intensified forms of rural poverty is explored in chapter 5.

Apartheid in retreat: reform and repression, 1974–90
By the mid-1970s, a government that had swaggered through the previous decade lost its step, stumbled – and never fully regained its balance or its confidence. There were three main components to the difficulties encountered by the regime: economic malaise, the return of internal resistance, and a shift in the regional balance of forces that called South Africa's security into question. These are summarised briefly below.

- The economic growth of the 1950s and 1960s generated its own contradictions. Low black wages meant a stunted domestic consumer market. Bantu education and job reservation ensured that African workers lacked the requisite skills. Then in 1973 the OPEC crisis saw oil prices treble, triggering an international recession. Growth slowed in almost all countries in the 1970s, and recovered in the 1980s – but the South African economy performed significantly worse than those of Asian, European, Latin American and other African countries: it was one of only a handful of economies worldwide in which GDP per head fell for the period 1973–94.

The last 20 years of apartheid witnessed inflation, stalled growth, soaring unemployment and a growing problem with the balance of payments.[5]

- Simultaneously, the apartheid state was suddenly confronted by militancy and mobilisation among black South Africans. A generation of angry university students formulated Black Consciousness; the Durban strikes of 1973 led with remarkable rapidity to a militant, independent trade union movement. Finally, in June 1976, police fired on marching school pupils in Soweto, triggering a youth uprising that ebbed and flowed for 15 months, cost over 700 lives, and galvanised entire communities. These strands of organised opposition recreated the possibility of mass-based protest politics, absent since Sharpeville.
- Caetano's right-wing regime in Lisbon fell in 1974. Portugal abandoned its African colonies, and Frelimo and the MPLA headed the governments of independent Mozambique and Angola. South Africa was no longer protected by a *cordon sanitaire* of white-ruled states. The exiled ANC could now seek bases for its armed wing, MK, in states neighbouring South Africa. An ill-judged invasion of Angola by South African troops began a decade of costly border war.

South Africa responded to this treble-layered crisis, under President P.W. Botha, with a 'slow, irresolute, pragmatic retreat' from the doctrinaire certainties of high apartheid.[6] Government mounted an ambivalent programme of authoritarian reform, trying to rescue and re-stabilise the apartheid project. It made some concessions: limited recognition of black trade unions; expanded rights for black urban 'insiders'; overtures to win support from a growing black middle class; and the ham-fisted experiment of the Tricameral Parliament. Simultaneously, the government sought to beef up both external defence and internal 'law and order' measures. Defence spending rose to almost 20% of the budget; the new National Security Management System effectively placed day-to-day administration under military control. Tocqueville, 200 years ago, observed that an authoritarian regime was at its most vulnerable when it attempted to reform – and the 1980s in South Africa provided a textbook instance.

Urban poverty and apartheid

Patterns of urban poverty changed dramatically under apartheid, because the cities themselves were transformed. Cities were the front line of apartheid, where a social war was waged between state power and demographic change. In the short term, state power prevailed. But by the closing years of apartheid rule, the state was in retreat, its policies in tatters and South African cities in key respects a zone of scorched earth.

In 1948, the immediate challenge to the NP government was to re-establish social and political control over the cities. In the eyes of NP politicians and their supporters (especially white workers), such control had slipped in several alarming ways: demographically, industrially, politically and with regard to housing. For a quarter of a century, since the 1923 Urban Areas Act, South African cities had become more segregated, but during the 1940s they also became far more difficult to control in the interests of white supremacy.

The growth of the black urban population was not only numerically substantial, but also – even crucially – significant for its changing composition. From the mid-1930s, the gender balance of urbanised Africans changed rapidly. By the late 1940s, men no longer predominated, as they had before. In 1936, women made up only 27% of Johannesburg's African population, but by 1951 they composed over 40%. The presence of women and children was the clearest indicator that the urban black family was a permanent presence in the cities. When the NP won the 1948 election, just under a quarter of the total African population was urbanised; but in absolute numbers this meant that 1.8 million Africans were living in towns and cities, matching – for the first time – the number of white townspeople.[7]

Another set of changes saw a rapid rise of African workers in the booming manufacturing sector, which during the 1940s came to employ more workers and earn a larger share of GDP than mining. Over 100,000 of the 125,000 workers who entered manufacturing and construction during the war were black. Their real wages rose, and they became more militant. By the end of the war the Council of Non-European Trade Unions claimed to have 150,000 members, and the number of hours lost to strike action increased fifteen-fold. Workplace activism was accompanied by community protests, notably in the Alexandra bus boycotts of 1943 and 1944, but also in a whole range of similar actions across the Witwatersrand.[8]

The area in which African protest actions most directly shook the state's control was a crisis in housing the burgeoning urban population. The crisis had several elements. One was the drastic over-crowding of the formal housing sector. The Smuts government built practically no new urban housing for Africans during the war years, and as a result many of the newcomers found accommodation as subtenants in the houses or backyards of local residents. Over-crowding was inevitable and, with space at a premium, 'rack-renting and cavalier treatment of tenants by landlords also became common'. Living conditions in these congested quarters were 'appallingly insalubrious … Poverty was pervasive and levels of malnutrition high … Outbreaks of diphtheria, tuberculosis, pneumonia and enteric fever were common.'[9]

By the end of 1946, some 63,000 people lived in Johannesburg's squatter camps alone. Similar incursions took place in other major cities. In Durban, by 1949 one-third of registered African male workers had no formal accommodation; shantytowns – the largest of which was Cato Manor – mushroomed. In Cape Town, 30 squatter camps housed an estimated 25,000 men and 5,000 families. By 1950 – Verwoerd told the Senate – the black squatter population in urban and peri-urban areas was estimated at 200,000. Conditions in these squatter camps were dire. Those who took their chances by seizing and protecting pockets of illegal space mainly came from 'the poorest sections of the urban population', and material deprivation, insecurity and social instability were common in all the major squatter communities.[10]

Faced with urban influx and housing policies in disarray, the apartheid state sought, firstly, to restrict African access to the cities; and, secondly, to contain, control and discipline those who were granted permission to remain. Its weapons for the first aim were pass laws, police raids, Section 10 rights and the rest of the influx control apparatus. The crucial means to the second aim was the construction of new African townships – arguably 'the key institution of segregation and apartheid'.[11] A massive state housing programme through the 1960s and 1970s created an urban geography that still dominates contemporary South Africa, 'an archipelago of relentlessly impoverished "suburbs" quarantined in their "buffer zones" on the outer fringes of white towns and cities'. Living conditions in the townships constitute the 'central material fact in the daily lives of a majority of South Africa's urban population' – an observation as true today as when it was made 25 years ago.[12]

South Africa's townships were parented by planners and politicians: their form, funding and function were the outcome of a convergence between planning and architectural modernism and the NP's desire for comprehensive segregation. The concept of regular, purpose-built residential areas, separated from commerce and industry by green belts, was a staple of mid-century modernism in Europe and North America. Distinctive South African features – in addition to their segregated raison d'être – included site-and-service provision allowing for temporary accommodation until permanent housing was available; construction work carried out by poorly paid black artisans; services such as water and roads funded by a tax on employers; and a driving concern for houses that were as cheap as possible. How orderly housing served the apartheid project was spelled out by Verwoerd in 1952. Cities were blighted by 'squatter chaos, overcrowding of existing Native plots, illegal lodging in white yards, … [and the presence of] those who refuse to work and thus don't belong in the city'. He proposed a solution. The social ills could 'only be combated once large enough legal townships for Natives are established close to the towns … an adequate distance from the European town', separated 'by an industrial buffer' and 'at a considerable distance from main … roads'. That 'Bantu townships' served a political purpose as well as a housing function was thus made clear. 'Orderly housing is a prerequisite of proper control

... This scheme [is] to house all workers under control.' [13]

Soweto is the classic instance of what were called the 'new model townships'. These were tightly controlled and segregated spaces, designed for optimal surveillance; they housed black workers whose energies were spent in white factories or institutions; they had none of the resources, complexity or variety of real cities. Their architecture was notoriously uniform and drab; but there was a purpose to the grid of streets with identical houses. Township housing assumed a single, orderly, nuclear family. A township house was meant to be the antithesis of the 'spatial chaos, disorder and moral degeneracy' associated with squatter communities and older locations.[14] The construction of mass housing in the townships was an essential element of the apartheid project: if some Africans were to be permitted to live in the cities, they should be housed in circumstances which would make them responsible, hard-working family members.

What did the new model township signify for urban poverty? Three broad trends can be identified: limited material and welfare improvements for their residents; the creation of a particular urban environment marked by alienation and violence; and, over time, a growing income and social differentiation within the black urban population. With respect to the first of these, especially in the 1950s for many of the new residents – notably those moved from squatter camps or from backyard shanties – the rented housing was hugely welcome, representing 'an escape from the unbearable overcrowding, lack of basic facilities and exploitation by rack-renting landlords'. Other tenants resented the poor quality of the buildings, their distance from the workplace, and their limited facilities. Particularly in the site-and-service schemes conditions were even more meagre than in the cheaply built 'matchbox' houses.[15]

In terms of material conditions and welfare, townships provided a more uniform standard of living than in the volatile and socially fluid squatter camps, freehold areas and backyard tenancies. In the 1950s and early 1960s, the great majority of black urban wage earners were unskilled, their income barely enough to meet subsistence needs. The greater stability provided by urban life was reflected in life expectancy and child mortality rates. Life expectancy for Africans rose from 40 for those born in 1945 to 60 for those born in 1985 (the latter figure, it should be noted, roughly that reached by white South Africans in the 1930s).

A second general aspect of life in the townships was the creation of a starkly limited form of urbanisation – indeed, apartheid townships created a kind of anti-city. They concentrated huge numbers of residents in high-density living, but without even basic civic facilities. That extreme income poverty decreased in the townships is indisputable; but it has to be set alongside what David Dewar has usefully dubbed 'experiential poverty'. Historically, 'the genius of city areas' has been that they provide 'a range, variety and richness of activities and opportunities'. By contrast, townships provided very poor access to utilities, public space, work opportunities and entrepreneurialism; schooling, civic services and transport were strikingly deficient.[16] Of course, township residents were extraordinarily adept at improvisation and invention, finding ways of ameliorating life in these circumstances. Their resilience, cultural resources and social complexity have been wonderfully evoked by Jacob Dlamini (although it is worth noting that he was born in 1973, and he describes the final years of apartheid as lived in Katlehong).[17]

The anomie and precariousness of township life were experienced most acutely by people who were relocated by the Group Areas Act or by the destruction of their previous communities. While we should not romanticise life in Sophiatown, District Six or Cato Manor, they and similar areas had been the 'arteries through which the lifeblood of an older popular urban culture had been developing'.[18] What people lost through forced removals was a sense of community, existing networks of reciprocity and support, opportunities for informal income – all difficult to quantify. When John Western interviewed coloured families Group Area'd out of Mowbray onto the Cape Flats, he concluded that for some 'their physical housing conditions did improve' but there was no assimilation and only limited social mobility. All those he interviewed 'lost an intangible sense of community when they left Mowbray and gained in return a climate of fear'. Fear, because of crime: there was, remarked Erika Theron, a direct relationship between the removal of coloured people from one area to another and the development of criminal gangs.[19]

The third major feature of township life was class formation and social differentiation. The black urban population during apartheid saw, on the one hand, the growth of more skilled and better-paid workers and the emergence of a middle class; and, on the other hand, persistent forms of poverty expressed in over-crowded dwellings, illegal sublettings and the erection of backyard shacks. Although these processes accelerated during the 1980s, they affected urban life from the mid-1960s on. When the NP took power in 1948, there was only a tiny African 'middle class' in towns and cities: it comprised predominantly professionals such as lawyers, teachers, nurses, clergymen and the like. By the mid-1970s, the number of such 'salaried employees and businessmen' had grown to 94,000. There was also 'a new elite of public servants' and the beginnings of managerial and entrepreneurial elites, as Africans moved into administrative and retail niches within the townships. Owen Crankshaw has provided a detailed account of the changing labour market in the 1970s and 1980s, which saw Africans moving into white-collar jobs and certain skilled and semi-skilled positions within manufacturing.[20] As discussed in chapter 5, in the aggregate these gains were offset by rising unemployment and structural poverty; but for the beneficiaries of new opportunities, there was a long-term escape from poverty. Their upward mobility was assisted by policy changes, especially those encouraging home ownership by Africans.

In summary: apartheid affected urban poverty in different ways. It commenced by removing squatter communities and flushing out much of the backyard lodger population from existing housing. It proceeded to remove entire older settlements, in every major city: Sophiatown, Pageview, District Six, Cato Manor, South End, Lady Selborne and North End among others. Those displaced by all categories of urban removals were housed in 'new model townships', designed and built to house a biddable and obedient population, a source of cheap labour, socially and politically neutered. Township life meant material improvements for some residents at the cost of relentless surveillance and bureaucratic controls: 'the environment was alienating, anonymous, and harsh, conducive to casual and violent interchanges and the very opposite of what apartheid ideologues had imagined might develop into peaceful, family-based "native villages"'.[21] And there is a profound historical irony: the entire apartheid project was eventually mortally wounded by mass unrest in the country's townships, exactly where the planners had hoped to impose maximum control. This part of the story is told in the next chapter.

5

Social engineering, rural destitution and mass unemployment

'When you are out of job, you realise that the boss and the government have the power to condemn you to death. If they send you back home (and back home now there's a drought) and you realise you can't get any new job, it's a death sentence. The countryside is pushing you into the cities to survive, the cities are pushing you into the countryside to die.'
– Migrant worker, quoted by Michael Savage

The two defining features of rural poverty that existed before 1948 continued, and intensified, through the apartheid years. The long-term degeneration of the reserves accelerated from about 1960, as the disparity deepened between the population they housed and their ability to meet food and other requirements. Families of farm labourers continued to subsist on the lowest wages of any sector of employment. Even while their earnings remained artificially low, these workers came under acute new pressures, leading by the 1970s and

1980s to mass evictions. But in addition to these existing aspects of rural impoverishment, there were other, unprecedented policies and processes that condemned large numbers of people to poverty, many of them in grotesque institutional settings.

Apartheid and poverty in the reserves

The areas successively known as native reserves, homelands, Bantustans and 'self-governing states' had long housed a migrant workforce. The artificially low wages paid to miners and other city workers were justified on the grounds that supposedly 'tribal' migrants had homes in the reserves, which sustained their families. The ability of reserve dwellers to produce a proportion of their own food requirements appears in most cases to have remained fairly stable until the 1950s, although subsistence finally rested on the institution of migrancy and remitted wages, and agricultural production was already under severe pressure. The Tomlinson Commission, appointed to advise on policy towards the reserves, reported in 1956 that only a small sector of the reserve peasantry had escaped extreme poverty, and that urgent steps were required to develop these regions. Its recommendations for an ambitious – and expensive – programme of economic rehabilitation and development were rejected; Verwoerd instead continued the existing 'betterment' schemes and sought to strengthen the authority of traditional chieftaincies.

Living conditions in the reserves/Bantustans deteriorated significantly over the next 20 years. This was largely because their population increased dramatically: a product of natural population growth and of the forced relocation of families and communities from cities and white-owned farms – an aspect of the social engineering discussed below. The average population density of the reserves almost doubled between 1955 and 1969. The total amount of food produced remained steady, but per capita food production fell steeply. Rising population figures meant that growing numbers of families had no access to arable land; there were also households who had been allocated small plots but owned no cattle and were unable to plough. 'The majority of households in the reserves were only part-time farmers, predominantly women and elderly persons' without the land or resources to produce even their subsistence needs: 'poverty-stricken rural communities were highly dependent on remittances ... pensions, and other income transfers'.[1]

By the early 1980s, a series of detailed local surveys and analyses of the Bantustans[2] revealed not only regional variations but also some clear general trends. These included high levels of malnutrition and poverty-related diseases (for instance, in a Gazankulu clinic at Mhala, 63% of admissions to the children's ward were due to seven diseases associated with poverty); rising numbers of female-headed households among the relatively poor population; a rapidly growing proportion of the population without land and cattle; and, consequently, a sharp increase in income inequality among the population. While a majority of households had rising absolute incomes (from a very low base), the poor became poorer, both relatively and absolutely, because of landlessness and unemployment.[3]

The immediate cause of rising landlessness, inequality and persistent poverty was rapid population increase in areas already underdeveloped and disadvantaged, historically unable to feed themselves, and structurally dependent on the sale of labour power to mines, factories and farms. Accelerated population growth, in turn, was partly an outcome of natural population growth and partly due to government policies of 'separate development', which morphed, as 'grand apartheid', into Bantu Authorities. Verwoerd's Promotion of Bantu Self-Government Act (1959) was premised on the claim that 'the Bantu people ... do not constitute a homogeneous people, but form separate national units', and that they should therefore exercise 'self-government' in each of eight [later ten!] designated ethnic units. The underlying rationale was that bestowing 'the Bantu' rights in an ethnic enclave was a justification for denying them any political rights at all in 'white' South Africa. The central fallacy of this specious reasoning was that the territories identified as homelands were simply the old 'native reserves', several of them geographically fragmented, all of them desperately poor.

In 1976, the Transkei became the first of four 'independent' Bantustans. The logic of grand apartheid had been taken to new extremes. Legislation in 1970 provided that *every* African was to become a citizen of one or other homeland – whether a person had ever lived in that homeland or not. Transkei, Ciskei, Bophuthatswana and Venda were all ushered into fictive independence with new flags, stamps, anthems and other trappings of Ruritanian statehood. Their 'citizens' automatically lost their South African citizenship. Connie Mulder, Minister of Plural Relations and Development, congratulated himself in 1978: 'If our policy is taken to its logical conclusion ... there will not be one black man with South African citizenship ... Every black man in South Africa will eventually be accommodated in some independent new state in this honourable way.'

Social engineering and rural destitution

This elaborate exercise of devolving limited powers to those 'traditional' authorities willing to collaborate was a counterpoint to the central challenge confronting apartheid politicians and planners: restricting the number of African families in the cities. If apartheid was to control the flow to the cities, it had somehow to dam the tides from the countryside. This was the social equivalent of making water flow uphill. It could only be achieved by determined and ruthless social engineering. Social engineering means altering economic or social behaviour according to political objectives. More prosaically, but equally accurately, it means pushing large numbers of people around, compelling them to do things they would not otherwise have done. Deborah Posel, who calls the process 'economic engineering', reminds us that a deliberate policy 'with the goal of racializing access to resources, property and wealth, within the rubric of a capitalist economy, was one of the striking singularities of the apartheid project'. In particular, apartheid planners were determined to find new solutions to the perennial problem of keeping African urbanisation under control. Verwoerd and his planners knew that the 1950s approach – trying to minimise numbers by influx control – had failed. Instead, during 'apartheid's second phase, removals were used to excise large chunks of the urban African population altogether'.[4]

Because women were seen as the key to urban family life, apartheid's social planners were determined to limit the numbers of women in towns and cities. In the grim language of General Circular no. 25 of 1967, it was 'accepted government policy that the Bantu are only temporarily resident' in white cities. Therefore, people who became 'for some reason or another, no longer fit for work or superfluous for the labour market' would be relocated, to one of the Bantustans. Those 'who are normally regarded as unproductive and as such have to be resettled in the homelands' included 'the aged, the unfit, widows, women with dependent children'. The

Table 5.1: Results of social engineering: distribution of African population (%)

Year	Urban areas	White-owned farms	Bantustans
1960	29.6%	31.3%	39.1%
1970	28.1%	24.5%	47.4%
1980	26.7%	20.6%	52.7%

assault on Africans' residential rights in the cities meant that the proportion of the total African population living in cities actually *fell* during the 1960s and 1970s. The share of the total African population living in the Bantustans rose from just under 40% to over 50% (see Table 5.1). This was social engineering with a vengeance. Altogether, nearly 1.6 million people were subjected to forced removals from the cities: either in terms of the Group Areas Act or decanted as 'surplus' to one or other 'homeland' reserve.

The Bantustans continued to be vast dormitories of migrant labourers. But they served a further function during 'high apartheid'. They became the dumping grounds of apartheid, receptacles for 'the discarded people' or 'surplus people'.[5] Those endorsed out of the cities as 'superfluous for the labour market' were only a small fraction of the estimated 3.5 million people forcibly relocated. The largest single category of removals comprised families evicted from white-owned farms – discussed below – and they were among some 3 million

Table 5.2: Estimated numbers of forced removals, 1960–83

Farm evictions	1,129,000
'Black spot' removals and 'consolidation'	614,000
Urban removals	730,000
Group Areas	860,000
Informal settlements	112,000
Infrastructure/strategic	103,500
Total	3,548,900

people added to the already congested Bantustans (see Table 5.2).

The dreaded 'GG' (Government Garage) lorries that came to symbolise forced removals decanted their human cargoes into one of half-a-dozen different sorts of relocation areas. The bleakest of these were the desolate resettlement camps, first described by the Catholic priest Cosmas Desmond. He visited and wrote about a 'labyrinth of broken communities, broken families and broken lives', casualties of forced removals, 'homeless prisoners … in their own land'.[6] The classic 'resettlement camp' consisted of 'a collection of tin or wooden temporary huts (or tents) … tucked away in some remote and impoverished corner of a Bantustan … distinguished by their extreme poverty, their very dense population (mainly women, children and old people) and their tin toilets'.[7] There were several hundred such places, each a beacon of despair.

Resettlement camps and transit camps were intended to be temporary (although some became permanent). Other types of relocation settlements were spelled out in the Lewis Carroll language of apartheid bureaucrats ('when I use a word', said Humpty-Dumpty, 'it means just what I want it to mean'). The most common category was 'closer settlements', designed to house families moved from farms, black spots and mission farms, and expected to construct their own dwellings; 'agricultural settlements', which provided tiny plots with separate communal farming land; 'rural townships' for 'families whose breadwinners are usually employed in White areas ... or for the aged, widows, women with dependent children etc.'; and 'full-scale replacement border townships ... planned and developed in a sophisticated way', located so that workers could commute daily into 'white' areas.[8] What this elaborate taxonomy actually yielded was 'displaced urbanisation': the concentration of millions of black South Africans, in the 1970s and 1980s, into 'huge rural slums'. These were politically in the Bantustans, but economically just near enough to metropolitan labour markets to make commuting possible. Statistically, they were densely populated enough to show up in census data as urban; but because of the total absence of proper urban infrastructure, services or jobs, it is accurate to regard them as new sites of rural poverty.[9]

Botshabelo, which is within commuting distance of Bloemfontein, was bare veld in 1979; ten years later it held half a million people. The Winterveld area of Bophuthatswana, from where commuters could reach the Pretoria-Brits-Rosslyn labour market, held 750,000 people. Joe Lelyveld, of the *New York Times*, had visited each of the ten homelands and seen most of the major 'closer settlements'. And so he did not expect to be surprised when he revisited Kwaggafontein in KwaNdebele. Yet the visual shock of what had happened in two and a half years staggered him. 'It was no longer just a spot in a rash of "closer settlements". Now it was a part of a nearly continuous resettlement belt ... [for 40 miles] a serpentine stream of metal shanties and mud houses ... Such sights can be seen in other countries, usually as a result of famines or wars. I don't know where else they have been achieved as a result of planning.'[10]

Changing labour market and mass unemployment

There was another form of acute rural poverty. It is flagged by the statistic that between 1960 and 1980 the proportion of Africans living on white-owned land fell from 31.3% to 20.6%. In 1960, one in three black South Africans lived on land owned by whites, often on land which had belonged to their forefathers. By 1980, just one in five did so. There were two main categories of families who lost their toe-hold on the land. Firstly, many unskilled farm workers were given notice to leave as commercial agriculture mechanised. Farmers using tractors and harvesters no longer relied on part-time work by labour tenants. In 1947, only 22,000 tractors were used on South African farms; by 1961 there were 122,000, and by 1980 over 300,000. Farmers simply laid off their resident workers – on maize farms, perhaps 70% of seasonal workers and 50% of those who had lived all their lives on the farm.

Secondly, there was a concerted effort by government to expunge any remaining tenancies, especially labour tenancies, sweeping away the last vestiges of an African peasantry living on white-owned land. White farmers who were mechanising now objected to the institutions of sharecropping and labour tenancy – 'mainstays of rural African families for many decades' – and the state moved to eradicate them.[11] Families displaced by this pincer movement of economics and politics frequently wound up as members of the underclass in rural closer settlements; by the 1980s, many made their way to the cities, in search of a site in an informal settlement and, hopefully, a job or an opportunity for informal earnings.

The pressures on farm workers and tenants illustrate an important point. During the apartheid years, people experienced poverty in different ways. In broad terms, they became poor either as a direct result of policies or as an indirect result of economic change during apartheid. People impoverished by apartheid policies included families who lost inner-city homes and were moved to bleak, alienating and violent new townships; and those who were forcibly relocated to resettlement camps or to zones of displaced urbanisation. In the homelands, apartheid policies created an underclass of the landless, unskilled and unemployed, no longer wanted by farmers or on the mines, lacking any safety net in subsistence agriculture and without the kinds of networks that might lead to jobs.[12] Farm workers laid off as agriculture mechanised were poor to start with, but many were plunged into destitution, essentially as a result of economic and technological change.

But by far the most important form of poverty arising from economic change was structural unemployment on a massive scale. The changing economy has been extensively analysed elsewhere:[13] I can only offer the briefest summary. In the 1960s, industrial manufacture and the service sector expanded. To fill the jobs needed, employers and government edged away from job reservation. A permanently urbanised, better-educated and more skilled African working class emerged in the cities – and its members moved up the skills and wages ladder. Employers reorganised their activities in accordance with a shift from an unskilled to a semi-skilled and skilled labour force. They raised wages, yes; but they also moved from labour-intensive to capital-intensive production. They mechanised where they could; invested in the most skilled workers available – and laid off unskilled labour. So, for African workers with relevant skills, with secondary education and with Section 10 rights, the 1960s and 1970s were years of rising income and the emergence of a black middle class. Similarly, the mining industry moved decisively away from a migrant workforce characterised by high turnover and low skills towards a 'career' mine labour force of relatively skilled and experienced workers.

In both instances, the relative security of a skilled and semi-professional elite was the mirror image of the acute vulnerability of the unskilled. No longer required by manufacturing or the mining industry, unskilled men joined those expelled from the agricultural sector to constitute a massive army of the unwanted. They lived in 'closer settlements', in sprawling rural slums like Botshabelo, or in the shack peripheries of cities and small towns. As Colin Murray poignantly observed in 1995, 'Their prospects are grim. Formal sector or stable employment is hopelessly beyond the reach of very many of the youth … they live by their wits from one day to the next; and they hone their skills as best they may in disparate nooks and crannies of the second economy. Energies are committed to pursuing tenuous scraps of opportunity; to negotiating the routine bureaucratic obstructions of a hostile state; to sustaining, against the odds, the fragile threads of family integrity.'[14]

Commencing in the 1970s, but gathering pace in the 1980s, the South African economy underwent an historic transition: a shift from labour shortages to a labour surplus, generating structural underemployment and unemployment. The rise in unemployment was rapid and dramatic. By the end of the 1970s, unemployment was increasingly visible, as men queued at labour bureaux, outside factory gates, and alongside countless urban streets and roads. They were the casualties of a convergence of two crucial developments: South Africa's dismal economic performance after 1973 and, by the 1980s, a shrinking GDP; and the tendency to replace labour by capital – on the mines, in agriculture and in manufacturing. Because the apartheid state kept such poor statistics, it is difficult to provide precise figures for structural unemployment, but Charles Feinstein's careful work yields an estimate that is reproduced in Table 5.3.

'Whatever its precise scale', he concludes, 'unemployment was clearly a human tragedy on a staggering scale.' By the end of apartheid, somewhere between 4 and 6 million people were unable to find work. Half the population lived in households with at least one unemployed adult. In half of those households, nobody held a formal job. And among those without jobs, less educated, less skilled and less urbanised people had very little prospect of employment, even in the mid- to long term. They experienced structural poverty in acute form.[15]

Townships in turmoil and new patterns of urban poverty
In the 1970s the government began to lose control of the townships, politically, administratively and socially. Political confrontation on the urban front line began of

Table 5.3: Estimates of structural unemployment, 1960 to 1996

	1960	1970	1980	1996
Employed	5,840,000	7,460,000	9,530,000	9,850,000
Unemployed	460,000	530,000	4,700,000	4,880,000
Ultra-discouraged workers (UDW)			1,400,000	1,400,000
Unemployed + UDW			5,100,000	6,280,000

course in Soweto, in 1976; and took new organisational form with the emergence from 1979 of 'civics', typically campaigning around housing, rents, transport costs and schooling – the civic associations became a major component of the United Democratic Front (UDF), launched in 1983. In September 1984, the Vaal Uprising exploded, igniting an urban insurrection that spread to Soweto and Eastern Cape townships. The UDF 'became a movement galvanised by local initiatives, with civics and youth congresses organising a remarkable series of consumer boycotts' to put pressure on city councils and local businesses.[16]

Financial pressures saw a substantial reduction in house building during the 1970s. While housing shortages fuelled urban protests, they also translated into new forms of poverty. There was a sharp rise of subletting, and a 'veritable mushrooming of informal residence'. Desperate rural people increasingly found ways of breaching influx controls, living in the cities as 'illegals', either as tenants in the backyards of township residents or as squatters in new shantytowns. In Cape Town, Crossroads was the best known of these 1970s settlements; it resisted attempts to remove it, and 'survived, grew, and developed a defiant and uncontrolled culture' which challenged the very premises of apartheid's urban regime. While squatting in the 1970s was semi-clandestine and relatively slow, the 1980s witnessed the mushrooming of open squatting, at times involving land invasions on the peripheries of existing townships.[17]

In the 1980s, the state tried to devolve housing and influx control powers to black local authorities – but the experiment backfired calamitously. The wave of protests and boycotts triggered by the Vaal Uprising demonstrated that in many townships there was no longer any effective authority. In 1986, pass laws were formally repealed, and it was announced that they would be replaced by a policy of 'orderly urbanisation'. Urbanisation certainly ensued; but it was far from orderly – what actually resulted was a convulsive disorderly urbanisation. Masses of people poured into the townships, many of them unskilled and unemployed refugees from the countryside. With ingenuity, determination and hope, they created new homes from whatever they could lay hands on. In Soweto, squatter settlements grew 'at a staggering rate' – by 1989 over 40,000 shacks had been erected. 'On every available piece of land stood groups of hovels and makeshift shelters.' Unsurprisingly, squatters were among the poorest Sowetans. In 1989, the average monthly income of a Soweto household was R900; over 20% of informal settlement households earned less than R300.[18] By the end of apartheid, the loss of control by the state was palpable: 'Townships no longer bear the hallmark of state control. Instead of the homogeneous landscape of official design ... almost every backyard hosts sub-tenants who live in shacks or formal outbuildings ... From the air ... the sheer volume of backyard shacks creates the impression of a residue of matchbox houses floating in a sea of shacks.'[19]

This scenario played out in all major urban areas. The population of greater Durban doubled between 1973 and 1988 – by 1988 it held 3.5 million people, about half of whom lived in shack settlements on the edges of the city. Most shack dwellers had jobs, so they were poor rather than destitute: but the settlements lacked the normal urban infrastructure of roads, sanitation, piped water and lighting. In East London, Duncan Village township housed 17,000 people in 1984. Then the floodgates opened. Six years later, the population was an estimated 80,000, many packed into shanties. In Cape Town, no new African housing was built in the 1960s and 1970s. Consequently, tenants crammed the backyards in Langa, Guguletu and Nyanga; and squatter settlements were erected wherever land stood vacant. This led to the creation of Khayelitsha, originally intended to be for formal housing – but a decade after its creation, shacks outnumbered formal houses three to one. Khayelitsha and informal settlements were estimated to hold three-quarters of a million people by the end of the 1980s – most of whom, it hardly needs saying, were desperately poor.[20] Structural poverty was predominantly located in the Bantustans initially; but with the collapse of influx control, it also found an urban presence in the shape of informal settlements.

This chapter has described the ruthless social engineering carried out under apartheid, and how it created new sites and forms of poverty in rural areas. It also outlined three linked processes: how an economy in crisis generated a new form of structural poverty; how its casualties left small towns and rural areas for the cities, living mainly in informal settlements; and how the apartheid state lost the ability to control population flows or maintain order in the cities. Social engineering was a leitmotif of apartheid's heyday; failing state machinery was a mark of its final years.

6

The ANC and social security
The good, the bad and the unacknowledged

This chapter explores a central aspect of post-apartheid policy with respect to poverty. It recounts the remarkable story of the social security programme developed by the ANC in government after 1994. As detailed below, it is remarkable in its scale; it is remarkable in the ways in which benefits are delivered; and it is remarkable for its economic, social and political salience. The social welfare cash transfers – pensions and grants – are the most effective mechanism of redistribution used by the ANC. Pensions and grants have stabilised livelihoods, sustained households and reduced destitution. They have translated materially into benefits for poor South Africans, and politically into high levels of voter support for the ANC in the poorest constituencies. A remarkable story: yet one that was entirely unanticipated in 1994, and that remains strangely unacknowledged by the ANC today. A brief account of how the ANC has described its social security policies when seeking election is instructive, and commences the analysis below. It is also a story more directly rooted in the past than many realise; its longer history goes back to the 1920s, and has shaped post-apartheid practices and policies quite fundamentally.

In 1994, the ANC ran an expensive, slick and effective election campaign. Among its political messages were a series of posters and press advertisements in which the echoes of the Freedom Charter were audible: 'Jobs, Houses and Education for All!', 'Land, Jobs and Education for All!' and the like. The anchor strapline for the whole campaign was *A Better Life for All* – and this was what the 1994 election manifesto was called. It promised everything one might have anticipated: public works, job creation, workers' rights, rural development, land reform, better education and health provision. But what about social welfare? A brief paragraph, headed 'Welfare and Pensions', promised a caring approach, special programmes for homeless children, an end to disability discrimination, and a commitment to old-age pensions. The only reference to welfare grants was this sentence: 'Pensions and grants due to people will be assured and allocated through post offices, banks, building societies or other outlets which are easy for rural people to use.' There was no hint here of a future massive expansion of existing welfare provision.

The manifesto had a much longer companion piece, the Reconstruction and Development Programme (RDP), running to over 150 pages. The RDP was essentially a wish list presented as policy proposals, a commitment to social transformation in broad, vague terms. On welfare and social security, it offered a little more than the manifesto, but not much more. 'Social security and social welfare' featured as the eleventh of eleven Basic Needs. Social security was defined as having two main components: social insurance schemes for employees and a 'social safety net'. Support from the safety net could come either in the form of cash or in-kind benefits, and would be focused on the disadvantaged. However, in a balancing act typical of the RDP, the Basic Needs chapter also warned: 'Although a much stronger welfare system is needed to support all the vulnerable, the old, the disabled and the sick who currently live in poverty, a system of "handouts" for the unemployed should be avoided.'

In 2004 the ANC's election manifesto – for the first time – claimed credit for having expanded social security provision: 'In 1994, social grants totalling R10-billion were distributed to 2.6 million recipients and they were based on race. Today government equitably distributes R34-billion in social grants to more than 7 million beneficiaries: the aged, young children in poor households, people with disabilities and others.' In 2009, these statistics were updated – but in the lengthy section

the Second World War, Hertzog resigned and Smuts headed a new government. There was a brief reformist urge during the early 1940s, variously described as liberal, social democratic and even radical, although a persuasive analysis depicts the reforms as bound up in centralising and modernising the powers of the state. The best known of the reform initiatives was one that did not succeed: the Gluckman Commission of 1942–4, which recommended a single, co-ordinated National Health Service, providing free health care to all South Africans – recommendations, said Smuts, 'for which the country is not ready'.[2]

Alongside Gluckman, there flowed a separate stream of support for an expanded welfare system. Smuts grumbled to a correspondent, 'I don't like all this preoccupation with the post-war paradise on earth … people talk Beveridge instead of war and Hitler.'[3] Some welfare reforms were implemented: most notably, the Pensions Act was amended to include Africans and Indians (at a value about one-quarter of that awarded to whites). Disability and invalid grants, and pensions for the blind, were also extended to all races. Deborah Posel sums up these reforms: 'What was imagined was a racialized welfare state' with racially differentiated benefits. The aims of the welfarist lobby 'were fully compatible with the maintenance of a system of white supremacy, albeit one with a much more human face'.[4]

This has a bearing, too, on the National Party's

election victory in 1948. Although the new government was preoccupied with racial separation, and ruthless when it came to social control, it shared with the welfare reformers an enthusiasm for a centralised and interventionist state. As John Iliffe puts it, 'Ironically, during the next forty years the National Party was to elaborate the most extensive welfare system in Africa, a system which, like the Apartheid programme, was born of urbanisation, inequality, state power, and rampant technocracy.'[5]

The new NP government did not abolish state pensions for black people. But during the heyday of apartheid – the 1950s and 1960s – the racial differentiation in the value of the pension increased. By the mid-1960s, the African old-age pension had fallen from being worth 25% of that paid to whites to only 13%. But the picture began to change in the 1970s as the regime was buffeted by acute economic strains and challenged by black political resistance. The government simultaneously beefed up its military and policing capacity, but also ditched such key elements of apartheid as the job colour bar and influx control. Alongside these statutory changes were less visible but equally important retreats from high apartheid. The annual budget began to redistribute resources from whites to blacks. More was spent on African schools, township infrastructure and public sector wages. From 1970 to 1993, the real value of pensions received by Africans rose by 7% a year while the numbers receiving it swelled from 400,000 to 1.5 million. In 1993, pension payments were de-racialised. All elderly South Africans received the same amount. Pension transfers had become the single most important instrument of redistribution, providing a major source of income for the poorest 20% of the population. At some point in the 1990s, pensions overtook migrant remittances as the most important source of income for rural African households.

In other words, using the fiscus as a means of redistribution – using taxes paid by the better-off to reduce the plight of the poor – was a well-established mechanism *before* 1994. A substantial reallocation took place during the last two decades of apartheid. Whites received 50% of total social spending (welfare plus education plus health care) in 1975, but only 32% in 1990 and about 16% in 1993. The ANC government elected in 1994 'inherited a budget that was already surprisingly redistributive'.[6]

The evolution of social protection policies since 1994
When it came to policy, the ANC in the 1990s began more or less from scratch. The early 1990s were a hothouse of policy development, with groups beavering away on draft policies for the economy, education, health, land reform, gender and much else.[7] Francie Lund has left a vivid account of how intensely she and her colleagues worked on social welfare policy, 'bridging the gap between vision

and provision', trying to win 'a race against time'.[8]

Once the ANC took office, policy formulation stepped up a gear. There were a plethora of commissions, committees and working groups, and in 1997 the welfare department published its White Paper for Social Welfare. All of these inquiries were strongly influenced by their context. Their authors were aware of the high levels of expectation among black South Africans. They knew that the AIDS epidemic meant that existing social and economic pressures were likely to worsen. And they were acutely aware of the utter disarray of welfare provisions in large parts of the country, most particularly the former Bantustans. There were 14 different welfare departments; several were riddled with corruption, fraud and inefficiency. 'Fusing this jumble of bureaucracies into a relatively coherent system', run by a single department, was an important achievement of the ANC's first term in office.[9]

Expansion

The massive growth in the provision of pensions and grants is the most obvious and most striking feature of the ANC government's policy and practice. In two decades – from 1994 to 2014 – the total number of recipients rose from 2.4 million to about 16 million. But it did not happen at once. Until about 2000, the total number of recipients rose only gradually. From 2000 it speeded up, but it has been since 2003 that the growth curve is steepest, the expansion fastest. As Figure 6.1 shows very clearly, most of the expansion was due to the numbers receiving child support grants and the doubling in the number of those receiving disability grants between 2000 and 2004 – an increase largely attributable to the HIV/AIDS pandemic.[10] The child support grant was the only category of grant added to the provision existing in 1994. It replaced the state maintenance grant, a much more generous grant, received by 200,000 women almost entirely from the coloured, white and Indian populations. The child support grant was worth only R100 a month when it was first introduced, but its growth was phenomenal, especially as the age of children eligible for the grant was raised. Between 2001 and 2011 the number of child support grants rose to 10 million, an increase of 1200% in the decade.

South Africa today has one of the world's largest social assistance programmes. Currently, nearly 18 million people – one of every three South Africans – receive a grant or pension. The ANC government spends about 3.5% of GDP on social protection, and among major countries in the global South this is unmatched in terms of expenditure or in terms of coverage. Although there have been constant concerns within the ANC about the cost of such programmes, government has permitted the expansion. This decision was 'linked to two quite fundamental predicaments': firstly, the radical deterioration of agrarian livelihoods in the ex-

Figure 6.1: Numbers of social assistance beneficiaries, 1994–2014, by programmes (millions), to end April annually[11]

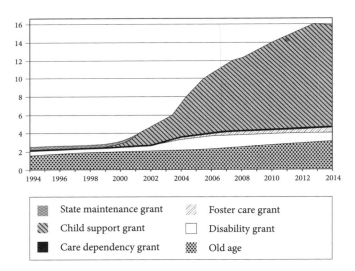

homelands; and, secondly, the failure of the ANC's economic policies to create jobs. Even between 2000 and 2008, when GDP grew at over 4% a year, this was largely 'jobless growth' and unemployment levels hardly budged. The simultaneity of these two crises, says James Ferguson, has brought an abrupt end to both of the 'great fantasies' about family life for black South Africans: the rural extended family providing for its members; and the urban nuclear family in which a male breadwinner played this role.[12]

Technology

Thanks to Keith Breckenridge, we know a good deal about the rise of South Africa's 'biometric state'.[13] For well over a century, successive South African governments have used the available technologies of identification to survey, police, record and control their citizens. The apartheid regime, from the early 1950s, implemented a massive project of fingerprinting as the basis of the Population Register. In the 1980s, fingerprinting as the prerequisite for identity documents was extended to whites. Come democracy – and these huge data banks made possible the mushroom growth of the cash transfer system.

The combination of biometric identification and smart-card payment of grants was piloted in the KwaZulu homeland a decade before it was rolled out nationally. In 1986, Chief Buthelezi appointed First National Bank (FNB) to undertake the registration and payment of pensions for KwaZulu. FNB formed a new company, which used fingerprint ID as the basis for payments. The bank had a vested interest in finding a way of reaching the millions of people currently outside the banking system.[14]

And precisely this technology provided the ANC with a ready-made solution when it surveyed the fragmented and inefficient welfare system. The Chikane Committee seized on biometric ID as essential for creating 'a uniform system for the country as a whole'. The 1997 White Paper followed this logic, calling for 'a National Social

Grants Register and automated fingerprint technology'. In 2004, a centralised agency responsible for welfare payments was created: SASSA – the South African Social Security Agency. And in March 2012 SASSA commenced the massive task of creating a biometric record – with fingerprint and voice recordings – for 18.9 million potential recipients of pensions and grants. The high-tech system of biometric identification and smart-card payments 'is a complex interchange between the state and citizen that occurs millions of times each month',[15] a digitised social contract. Biometric identity as the platform for delivering social protection has been welded into South Africa's machinery of state. There is, remarks Breckenridge, 'a sweet and perplexing irony' in that technology developed as a means of racial coercion under apartheid is today championed as a key weapon in addressing post-apartheid poverty.[16]

Architecture: size and shape of the welfare system
We have noted the massive expansion of welfare provision after 1994, and the technology that enabled it. But the change in its *size* did not involve any fundamental change in the overall *shape* of the welfare state. The only new grant was the child support grant, which replaced one so generous that its extension to African children would have been unaffordable. Otherwise, the system expanded through changes to the parameters for each grant: age of eligibility, income threshold for means testing, and

so on. The ANC inherited from the late-apartheid state a welfare system of quite generous benefits, paid for from direct taxation. Pensions and grants were targeted at the 'deserving poor': people unable to work because of age or infirmity, or because they cared for young children. The ANC expanded this legacy but did not re-engineer it. It may be an exaggeration, but Seekings and Nattrass make an arresting claim: 'If it had not inherited relatively generous old-age pensions, disability grants and the State Maintenance Grant ... the ANC government would probably not have introduced such programmes, and would probably not have taken up the Lund Committee's proposals to introduce the Child Support Grant.'[17] Changing the size but not the shape of the welfare system also meant that there was less incentive for the ANC to re-conceptualise the system, or to interrogate the assumptions underpinning its design.

Impact

The South African system of mass cash transfers has attracted considerable scholarly attention, with international and comparative studies alongside close-grained local inquiries.[18] There is a robust consensus that the system of grants works, that they have positive outcomes in the lives of impoverished and vulnerable people. They have ameliorated ultra-poverty or destitution. The proportion of adults falling into the very lowest of ten categories for living standards fell from

11% in 2001 to 1% in 2011. Since 2000, cash transfers have reduced the poverty headcount and the poverty gap quite substantially. Paid for by taxes, the grants have been significantly redistributive. Without pensions and grants, the income share of the poorest 40% of the population would have been 3.3% in 2006; with pensions and grants, it rose to 7.6%. Their benefits have been concentrated among the poorest 40% of the population. The grants have improved access to other social benefits, such as education and health care. They have improved the welfare not only of direct recipients but also other members of their broader households. Women receive the bulk of grants: 99% of child support grants and 70% of old-age pensions go to women.

And yet –

Shortcomings

South Africa's social security net has been flung wide; but, in Michael Samson's telling phrase, it has a very loose weave. Very large numbers of people without resources receive no social assistance at all. This is because the South African welfare system, as it developed from the 1930s, and as it was de-racialised in the 1980s and 1990s, was based on the design of social welfare in Britain, New Zealand and Australia. And like those models, it rested on certain mid-20th-century assumptions. These included: that most people of working age would be able to find jobs; that people in work would insure themselves against short-term unemployment through contributions; and that working people would help provide for their retirement through contributory pension schemes. Obviously, since 1994 none of these conditions has been met.[19]

The social security net of the classic Anglo-Saxon liberal model is not intended to provide for the long-term unemployed. And in South Africa, for decades the long-term unemployed have received virtually no financial support from the state or from private schemes. In particular, young men are almost entirely excluded from the system of welfare grants.[20] One in three South Africans of working age is unemployed, and they are overwhelmingly African and coloured men in their 20s and 30s, who have never had a full-time job. The other category excluded from assistance is unemployed women of working age who have no children. So for many young men and women, it is more feasible to live with parents or grandparents than to seek for nonexistent jobs. Perversely, in many households it is the disabled, the sick and the elderly who generate income, and not young men and women in the prime of their lives.[21] Perhaps it is not so much a loosely woven net as one with a great, jagged hole at its centre.

Ideology

How does the ANC think about social security? How does it understand and explain its policies? How accurately does its ideology describe its practices? In fact, ever since 1994 the ANC's thinking on welfare has been deeply ambivalent. A senior official in the Department of Social Development told a researcher that 'I think what we are creating is a kind of ambivalent and schizophrenic society when it comes to social grants'.[22] Although the ANC wants to reduce poverty, it is unwilling to acknowledge that cash transfers of pensions and grants have been arguably its most effective pro-poor policy. It is unwilling to do so because the dominant ideological position in government is socially conservative, shot through with anxieties about handouts and dependency and a 'culture of entitlement'. It actively repudiates any notion that welfare provision is here to stay, and probably here to grow. Said President Zuma in 2011, 'We cannot be a welfare state. We cannot sustain a situation where social grants are growing all the time and think it can be a permanent future.'[23]

But the ANC's determination not to be a welfare state predates Zuma's presidency. In his first State of the Nation address, Nelson Mandela spoke about his government's commitment 'to confront the scourge of unemployment, not by way of handouts but by the creation of work opportunities'.[24] His successor, President Mbeki, voiced the ANC's welfare ideology at its most paternalist and most censorious. 'Call me a Thatcherite', Mbeki goaded the Alliance Left at the public announcement of GEAR in 1996; and he certainly recycled the Iron Lady's moralising hostility to welfare dependency, her disdain for 'handouts', and her belief that what the poor really needed was discipline and self-improvement. Government must 'reduce the dependence of people on grants', said Mbeki; people must not think 'it is sufficient merely to hold out their hands and receive a handout'.[25]

The 1997 White Paper acknowledged the need for a social safety net, but defined it in terms of the 'special needs' of those unable to work. It called for community development programmes which would 'increase the capacity of individuals and families to meet their own needs'. The White Paper also introduced what became a central trope in the ANC's discourse on welfare: that government would practise 'developmental social welfare'. As critics have objected, the term appropriated 'a developmental discourse to serve conservative ends and legitimise the idea that social security depends on community self-help', shifting responsibilities from the state to poor communities. Certainly, the notion of a 'developmental social welfare' was often brandished in reductionist and rhetorical ways. To take one example from many: resolutions at the ANC's Polokwane conference in 2007 insisted that 'We are building a developmental state and not a welfare state given that in a welfare state dependency is profound' and 'Whilst many families have access to social grants ... many of these households and communities remain trapped in poverty, are dependent on the state, and thus unable to access the opportunities created by the positive economic climate.'[26]

It is worth recalling that Zola Skweyiya, Minister

of Social Development for two terms from 1999 to 2009, tried to contest this discourse on welfare in his party as best he could, from within. Upon taking office, Skweyiya's call for action marked a 'stark departure' from previous government utterances: 'Our social policies assume the ability of families and communities to respond to the crisis. Welfare has proceeded as if these social institutions are fully functional and provide the full range of social support that is required to restore the well-being of people. Such a "business as usual" approach cannot continue.' The Minister then appointed Vivienne Taylor, well aware of her social democratic views, to chair a Committee of Enquiry into a Comprehensive System of Social Security. A key recommendation was that government implement a basic income grant (BIG) worth R100 a month (to be phased in over a decade).[27]

Skweyiya championed the proposal, announcing in November 2001 that a BIG was an excellent idea that might be introduced in the next budget; six months later, he added optimistically that 'nobody disputes the call for a BIG'. He was wrong. Cabinet quickly distanced itself from the Taylor Committee's proposal. Trevor Manuel and Thabo Mbeki scoffed that it would make little difference – and anyway was too expensive. Skweyiya continued trying to persuade his colleagues to accept a BIG – but, as he recalled in 2011, 'There were those who remain violently opposed' to the idea. In 2006, he hinted that government was still investigating a universal transfer and that 'something like a BIG' would be debated at the ANC's policy conference in 2007. Trevor Manuel retorted that this would bankrupt the country.[28] Had Skweyiya not been Minister between 1999 and 2009, prevailing views within the ANC might well have seen a reduction in welfare provision. A recent overview of the politics and policies of welfare concludes that 'Zola Skweyiya played a central role in this drama, recruiting paternalistic conservatives in support of a broadly social democratic position'.[29]

The new politics of distribution

It may be illuminating to locate the BIG campaign in South Africa – now a rather exhausted campaign lacking traction – within the challenging and important work of James Ferguson. It is impossible to do justice to Ferguson here, but worth conveying a sense of his arguments. Across the global South, he points out – in Asia, Latin America and southern Africa – extensive welfare programmes have been created, targeting the poor, using cash transfers. The 'really big "development" story of the last twenty years', he says, is 'the rise and rise of social protection'. And these countries are tackling poverty by 'the startlingly simple device of handing out small amounts of money to people deemed to need it'.[30] Paradoxically, then, a distinctive version of the welfare state has emerged within the neoliberal global order: during an age of privatisation, marketisation and the retreat of the state. The new politics of distribution, says Ferguson, are 'avowedly (and ... on balance, genuinely) pro-poor ... "Pro-poor" and neoliberal – it is the strangeness of this conjunction'[31] that he explores. He has assessed the campaigns around the basic income grant in South Africa and in Namibia as a kind of logical extension of the politics of distribution.

There is a pragmatic case for the BIG, which uses the neoliberal language of 'investment in human capital' and 'empowering' the poor – enabling them to behave as proper neoliberal subjects, rationally pursuing their interests, taking risks, being entrepreneurial. A universal grant does not require the surveillance and means testing of conventional social assistance programmes. The neoliberal state would require 'no policing of conduct ... no social workers coming into homes – and no costly bureaucracy'. A monthly ATM payment, resting on the proof of a fingerprint or iris scan, requires only one question to be answered: have you been paid this month or not? The state is admirably 'slim', yet carrying out a substantial and beneficial economic intervention.[32]

A different argument for a universal grant might be regarded as the social democratic case. It amplifies the findings of economists: that 'a BIG represents an effective, economically affordable and economically beneficial policy instrument'[33] by focusing on the lives of those who would receive the grant, especially those currently not catered for by the social security net. This case has been made by many, but nowhere more lucidly than by Jonny Steinberg, in an account based on what he observed in Pondoland, when grants and pensions expanded in the early 2000s: 'Welfare brings life, not idleness to the worlds of the South African poor … People have money they didn't before and they want to spend it where they live. And so the enterprising begin selling everything, from building materials to airtime … Welfare also gives young people the means to work … With money in their pockets, people have the means to go out into the world and search. You can see on pension payout day that welfare brings people closer to the mainstream, closer to life. These are not days of shame or resignation. They are festive and generous days, days of laughter and good spirits. With money to spend, people are feeling at their most human.'[34]

Finally, a radical case for a universal income grant goes further than the humane version by seeing the direct distribution of grants 'not as charity but as liberation', validating and including those in society who have long been excluded or marginalised. It rests entitlement not upon need but upon citizenship. Citizens are entitled to the monthly grant 'precisely because they, as the nation's citizens, are the real owners of the country and its mineral wealth'. A BIG would be 'what is sometimes termed "a citizen's income", a rightful share of a common stock of wealth'.[35] For a universal grant to have a radical, emancipating potential, it must be uncoupled from the labour market; must abandon the fiction that grants should go only to those unable to work; and, instead, see their receipt as the 'emblem of full citizenship'.[36] Poor people, whose labour is no longer required, have acquired other kinds of power, says Ferguson: they have rights within a democratic regime whose mass political base is precisely the historically excluded poor.

* * *

This chapter has described what has been good about the ANC's social welfare policies since 1994 – especially the beneficial impact of a massively expanded provision. It identified the 'bad' aspect of its record as the failure to cater for the long-term unemployed, in an era when long-term unemployment shows no signs of diminishing. It has also argued that the ANC has been reluctant to acknowledge what it has achieved, and even more unwilling to acknowledge what remains to be done. It remains in denial about its own achievements, insisting that it does not favour a welfare state even while in the process of constructing one. The ANC's prevailing stance since 1994 – despite the efforts of people like Zola Skweyiya – 'was one that chided the poor for remaining poor, rejected BIG but was unable to resist pressure for major cash transfers to the poor'.[37] Unless it were to acknowledge this critique, the ANC government is unable ever to take the politics of distribution to another level.

Poverty and policy options in South Africa today

'What thoughtful rich people call the problem of
poverty, thoughtful poor people call with equal
justice a problem of riches.'

– R.H. Tawney

This book has tried to frame provisional answers to
questions such as: Why is there so much poverty in
South Africa? What are its key features? How did it
come about? It has outlined the history of poverty,
emphasising that it changed over time, and that it is
not a static, continuous phenomenon. Earlier chapters
traced the lasting scars left on the face of South African
poverty by colonial dispossession and coerced labour,
by systematic segregation, and by a capitalist system
distinctive for its reliance on cheap, rightless black
labour. By 1948, South African society was already
defined by high levels of poverty and inequality patterned
by race. Apartheid intensified these features, tightening
controls over the black majority and deepening white

privileges. South African capitalism in the 20th century was 'a prototypical example of inequality-perpetuating growth'.[1] In the late 20th century, the political economy of apartheid changed: growth stalled, the income of black urban 'insiders' rose, and there was a fundamental shift from labour shortage to labour surplus. The structural poverty of mass unemployment was a direct outcome.

Poverty in South Africa today is not a natural, or a given, condition but the outcome of the history sketched in previous chapters. All visible aspects of poverty – some of which are so familiar they are barely noticed – are historically formed. In some cases, poverty is the result of deliberate policy; in others, the outcome of neglect; and, in yet others, the unintended consequence of social and economic changes. This history meant that the ANC government elected in 1994 inherited a society in which 58% of all South Africans and 68% of Africans lived in poverty.* It also inherited a working age population in which nearly one in five or nearly one in three (depending on whether one uses a narrow or a broad definition of unemployment)* was jobless.

Since the early 1990s there has been a phenomenal growth of research into South African poverty, carried

* The distinction saturates the literature on poverty – even though many economists regard it as a misleading one. The 'narrow' or 'official' rate counts people as unemployed if they have *actively* sought work in the previous four weeks; the 'broad' count includes discouraged work-seekers, who want to work but are not actively seeking or who have lost hope. These rates are measured within the working age population: from 15 to 64 years.

out by the state, by international agencies, by banks and the private sector, by NGOs and activists, and by academic economists and social scientists. However, this explosion of measuring and quantification has *not* created a coherent, consensual account. Data and findings have been highly contentious; different household surveys use different measures; scholars and policy-makers must select from a 'bewildering array of poverty lines';[3] while economists using the same data sets have analysed and interpreted them differently. Indeed, 'orthodox' and 'heterodox' economists (or the academic right and left) 'agree about many of ... the "facts" to be explained' even while their analyses reach fundamentally different conclusions.[4]

Particularly during the Thabo Mbeki presidency, the debate over the extent and nature of poverty became highly polarised and confrontational. To take a single example: in 2004 Mbeki's government claimed that 2.1 million new jobs had been created; but, responded a critic, these gains were mainly in the precarious informal sector. 'Homemakers who help sustain themselves ... out of backyard vegetable plots or who keep a few chickens are part of the new employed class ... That vast army ... who stand forlornly on street corners for hire or who sell coathangers, rubbish bags or handfuls of sweets ... all add to this two million jobs figure.'[5] To navigate these waters, this chapter relies upon studies which acknowledge the contested nature of poverty knowledge, and between them provide the nearest we have to an authoritative, agreed analysis.[6]

What these studies reveal can usefully be divided into three periods: 1994–2001; 2001–2008; and 2008 to the present. Between 1994 and 2001, the ANC opted for fiscal orthodoxy, deficit reduction, the abolition of some tariffs and subsidies, and generally a conservative macroeconomic policy. Some economic sectors shed jobs: in agriculture, mining and manufacturing large numbers of low-skilled workers were laid off. Unemployment rose rapidly, both in absolute terms and as a proportion of the labour force: from 17% of the workforce to 24% on the 'narrow' count; and from 29% to 38% on the 'broad' count. This inevitably impacted on the number of people living in poverty. By 2000, approximately 1.8 million more South Africans were living on less than $1 per day than there were in 1995. The years 1994–2001 witnessed 'rising unemployment, rising income poverty, and rising income inequality, all in the context of a lacklustre performance in economic growth'.[7]

From 2001, the Mbeki government retreated somewhat from the rigorous limits of the Growth, Employment and Redistribution strategy (GEAR); it increased state spending on infrastructure and especially on welfare grants. Spending on welfare and social assistance accelerated from R30.1 billion in 2000/1, or 3.2% of GDP, to R101.4 billion, or 4.4% of GDP in 2008/9. These years – before the onset of the banking crisis in 2008 – saw the

South African economy grow at a faster rate than at any other period since 1994. The transfer of funds through pensions and grants reduced both the poverty headcount and the poverty gap. Without pensions and grants, the income share of the poorest 40% of the population would have been 3.3% in 2006; with pensions and grants it was actually 7.6%. To use a different metric: in 2002, 18% of all households reported that grants were their main source of income. By 2006, this had risen steeply to 30% of all households – and nearly half of the households in the poorest 40% of the population.

This overview, so far, has referred only to income poverty, or money-metric poverty. But there were other ways in which the standard of living and well-being of poor people were affected: especially by the provision of housing, clean water, improved sanitation, electricity and other services. There are of course valid critiques of such provision: the shoddy quality of housing and its distance from the workplace; the costs to township consumers for electricity and water, and resultant disconnections – but even accepting these, each Census since 1994 has shown significant, and in some instances spectacular, growth in assets and services. Indeed, 'the improvement in access to services and assets [since 1994] … had been much stronger than the improvements in money-metric poverty and inequality'.[8] In the cities, the scale at which 'housing, services and social welfare have been extended to poor families is probably unprecedented by contemporary international standards'. Without them 'there would have been much more sickness, homelessness, starvation, and general suffering in urban areas'. Given that the rich pay the greater part of local and central taxes, there was substantial redistribution from rich to poor through these mechanisms. In short, say Bhorat and Kanbur, there has been 'a remarkable shift of fiscal resources towards poor households in post-*apartheid* South Africa'.[9]

Inequality

It is impossible to discuss poverty in post-apartheid South Africa without also considering inequality and unemployment. The story of inequality is striking. Although an ANC government has been continuously in power, despite pro-poor measures that have made a modest dent in income poverty, South Africa became a more unequal society after the end of apartheid, not a more equal one. Between 1994 and 2008, inequality increased measurably. The Gini coefficient rose from 0.66 in 1993 to 0.70 in 2008.[10] Two factors, in particular, caused inequality to deepen. Firstly, income was increasingly concentrated at the upper end of the scale. In 1993, the wealthiest 10% of the population accounted for 54% of the country's income; but by 2008 their share had risen to over 58%. Over the same period, the share of the first five deciles – the poorer 50% of the population – dropped from 8.3% in 1993 to 7.8% in 2008.[11]

Secondly, by 2008 about half of the wealthiest 10% of the population was African. They shared in a post-apartheid tsunami of consumerism. New shopping malls, gated residential villages, conspicuous consumption of luxuries, and foreign travel signposted an accelerated and expanded affluence. In post-apartheid South Africa, affluence has been de-racialised – but poverty has remained stubbornly racialised. Not all Africans stayed poor; but the great majority of the poor remained African. This meant that inequality within the African population increased sharply: indeed, it has been the most important single variable in driving the overall measure of inequality upwards in these years. Murray Leibbrandt and colleagues noted that poverty had been reduced even while inequality increased, and suggested a possible reason: 'that tackling inequality is more complicated and politically contentious than tackling poverty, as the former implies a "rearrangement" of the positions of the poor *and* the rich ... whereas the latter only involves the socio-economic conditions of the poor'.[12]

What about the years since 2008? The respectable growth rates of the previous six years contracted as the international banking crisis exploded. While South Africa's own banks were largely immune from the toxic debts that crippled major institutions in the advanced capitalist countries, the ensuing slowdown in international trade led to a sharp fall in growth. But after the initial shock of 2008/9, when perhaps a million jobs were shed, in terms of poverty, inequality and unemployment the overall trends identified for the years 2001–8 appear to have continued to the present. Thus, the combination of social grants, housing delivery and the provision of services has continued to reduce, modestly but significantly, the proportion of people living in poverty. In 2014, the World Bank reported that redistributive measures had helped elevate 3.6 million people above a poverty line of roughly R750 per month. These are not grounds for complacency or celebration. About 20% of the population continues to live in extreme poverty, according to Statistics South Africa (and more by other counts). Some 2,700 informal settlements, mainly in cities, are home to 1.6 million households. The data on inequality are less clear-cut, but the level of inequality has either remained constant or dipped very slightly since 2010.[13]

Unemployment

But the greatest failure of the years since 2008 – and, indeed, the greatest failure of the whole period since 1994 – has been the persistence of very high levels of structural unemployment (see Table 7.1). Economic growth has not been fast enough (except for a few years in the mid-2000s) to create enough jobs to increase participation rates in the labour market. By the narrow definition, one in five of the labour force was out of work in 1994; by the same measure, in 2015 one in four was jobless.

Table 7.1: Rising unemployment rate, 1994–2015

	Labour force	Employed	Unemployed
On official/narrow count:			
1994	11,386,000	8,896,000	2,489,000 (22%)
2014	20,122,000	15,055,000	5,067,000 (25%)
On broad 'expanded' count:			
1994	11,386,000	8,896,000	4,707,000 (35%)
2014	20,122,000	15,055,000	8,157,000 (35%)

If one uses the expanded definition of unemployment, to include 'discouraged workers', unemployment in 2015 reached 36.1%, a staggering figure, meaning that one in every three members of the labour force was without formal employment. In May 2016, Statistics South Africa released figures updating these rates to 26.7% and 36.3%.

Four other aspects of contemporary poverty are too important to omit, even if they can only be dealt with very briefly here. Firstly, the size and intractability of unemployment as a social ill tend to mask the problem of people who have jobs but still experience poverty. 'Although not often recognised, South Africa has both an unemployment problem and a working poverty problem.' Roughly 20% of South African workers live in households that are not able to meet their basic minimum food and non-food requirements. So while 'unemployment is the main concern for about half of the poor population ... low earnings or the poor quality of work is the concern for the other half'. 'Every day millions across South Africa do arduous work in jobs that cannot keep them and their dependants out of poverty. These are the "working poor" and according to a new study, there are about 5.5 million of them.' In 2014 there were some 13.1 million employees in the labour market – of whom half earned less than R3,224 per month. Domestic workers and farm workers earn by far the least, with the median wage at R1,577 and R2,253 respectively.[14]

Secondly, there is under way a shift between rural poverty and urban poverty. Historically, poverty in the countryside – in the reserves, on farms and in small towns – has tended to be more pervasive and more acute than poverty in cities and larger towns. It remains the case that 53% of working-age people in cities are in work, compared with only 29% in the former homelands. And only one in seven urban households relies mainly on social grants for income, compared with one in three rural households. Even so, a study published in 2010 demonstrated that 'While rural poverty rates remain substantially higher than those in urban areas, urban poverty rates are rising and rural rates seem to be falling ... [since 1994] poverty incidence barely changed in rural areas, while it increased in urban areas.'[15] The main dynamic at work in this change is that young adults are deserting the countryside, moving to the cities, where most of them swell the ranks of the urban poor. They struggle to get a foothold in the labour market; they are ineligible for social grants; and they are not on official waiting lists for housing.[16] In rural communities, there are higher proportions of the elderly and children than in the cities – and it is the elderly and children who are the main beneficiaries of cash transfers.

Thirdly, describing poverty at a very general level tends to overlook the complexity of the phenomenon. This can be illustrated by Anton Harber's vivid study of Diepsloot, north of Johannesburg, which was transformed in just over a decade from semi-rural, sparsely populated land to a dense, seething and contested informal settlement. As Harber says, from the news media 'you are likely to know this as a haven for criminals, a place of street justice, and a focal point of the 2008 outbreak of xenophobic violence'.[17] However, in contrast to this description, Harber conveys a compelling sense of Diepsloot's complex character. 'Each time I visited … I saw some nuance, some new detail which disrupted the pattern I thought I had seen the day before.'[18] While not ignoring its deprivation and violence, Harber also introduces us to savvy, hard-working community leaders and activists, politicians who are 'responsible, thoughtful, cautious and concerned'. He goes out at night with one of the volunteer patrols involved in community policing, men and women, young and old, out every weekend night to fight crime. He describes the street traders: 'At the side of every street, down every nook and cranny, there is someone selling something to make a living.' And he sits in while locals and foreigners negotiate an agreement as to the number of shops each may open, so as to avert further xenophobic violence[19] from erupting in Diepsloot.

Fourthly, any account of poverty should recognise the agency of the poor – as Harber does for the residents of Diepsloot. Poor people are not just statistics or casualties bobbing about in a sea of poverty; they are also active in shaping their lives. Marginalised and poor people in South Africa display a wide range of 'the arts of survival', devising livelihood strategies that are flexible, resourceful and largely invisible. They are involved in 'highly complex networks of reciprocal exchange'; they juggle credits and debts, derive income from a mix of formal and informal sources. These skills require 'knowledge, know-how, connections, experience, co-operative ability and an ability to negotiate conflictual terrain, eke out meagre resources, spot transient opportunities and bend them to one's purpose.'[20]

Policy options

The extent and severity of poverty are all too evident. But what can be done? What are the available policy options in order to reduce poverty, inequality and unemployment? These questions are pursued through a set of rather obvious policy options.

'Pro-poor' economic growth

During its first decade in office, the ANC appeared to regard economic growth as a panacea for poverty. It proceeded on the blithe assumption that integration into global capitalism and freeing up the corporate sector would guarantee growth, and that the benefits of growth would trickle down to the poor. As we have seen, that simply didn't happen, and during Mbeki's second term policy was recalibrated. Since 2006, successive ANC programmes have recognised that growth is necessary but not sufficient: benefits of growth must be *shared*. The Accelerated and Shared Growth Initiative in 2006 was followed by the National Industrial Policy Framework (2007), the Medium Term Strategic Framework (2009), and then the New Growth Path (2010). These provided variations on a couple of common themes: a 'developmental state' would support labour-intensive projects; an Expanded Public Works Programme would create work opportunities; infrastructure projects would be undertaken both for job creation and to support the economy, financed through more progressive taxation and the use of domestic savings in pension funds. In 2012, the National Development Plan (NDP, now official ANC policy) proposed a different way of tackling the unemployment crisis. It calls for a 'social accord' in which workers would accept wage rises lower than productivity increases (thereby increasing the profit share of the national income and decreasing that of wages); while in exchange business would reinvest profits in job-creating ways and restrain executive pay.[21]

An alternative model of growth-led poverty alleviation comes from the Congress of South African Trade Unions (COSATU) and the Left. This calls for policies that promote high-wage, high value-added production. It is linked to a call for a national minimum wage significantly higher than the current sectoral minimal levels. The core argument is that wage-led growth would stimulate domestic demand and consumption, so that the GDP grows faster. The policy package envisaged would include more public investment, and investment generally directed into the productive sector; expanding social protection to provide some relief to unemployed adults; limiting financial market speculation and curbing the huge sums that the conglomerates spirit out of the country annually; and introducing a wealth tax (like that advocated by Thomas Piketty).[22]

Yet all the variants of a policy dependent on growth to alleviate poverty face a fundamental problem. The GDP growth rates required to reduce unemployment significantly are relatively high – far higher than South African economic performance has been for years: there 'is a persistent, significant gap between the required … and the actual growth rate'. One economist has characterised waiting for high growth as 'waiting for Godot', arguing that far greater attention should instead be paid to developing the informal sector. Little, if any, policy effort has gone into making the informal economy a job-creating and employment-intensive component of the overall economy. Policies geared entirely to trying to 'fine-tune and turbo-boost' the formal economy in order to absorb more labour are fundamentally constrained; at some point they become 'less and less productive, even futile'.[23]

Job creation

Other than employment opportunities as a result of economic growth, government can also create jobs directly, through public works or public employment projects. The Reconstruction and Development Programme (RDP) was enthusiastic about the role of public works in reducing poverty; but for the first decade after 1994, the emphasis was almost exclusively on formal sector jobs. There were some, limited success stories of public works programmes: Kader Asmal's Working for Water project was one; some provincial governments have used labour-intensive forms of road maintenance and construction – but the list is not a long one.

After the 2003 Growth and Development Summit, the government agreed to expand public works programmes significantly, and an Expanded Public Works Programme (EPWP) was launched. In its first ten years, the EPWP created 5.3 million work opportunities. But it is important to recognise the differences between the short-term 'work opportunities' created by EPWP and formal sector employment. Work opportunities are not new jobs. The average duration of a work opportunity in infrastructure EPWPs was 65 days. And one has to ask, what precisely are PWPs intended to achieve? If it is a pathway into formal sector jobs, their record is patchy at best. If it is the transfer of skills and assets, not many projects have achieved that. While earlier policy documents saw EPWP as having an important role in labour-absorbing infrastructure projects, the National Development Plan limits their role to community-based services and mopping up surplus labour in the short term.

Here is a thought exercise: think back to the 1920s and 1930s, when the Pact and Fusion governments effectively solved the 'Poor White problem' – which had at its core unemployed and low-skilled white workers. The first element of the solution was the 'civilised labour' policy, protecting unionised workers: it is eerily reminiscent of COSATU's call for 'decent work'. The second element was an ambitious programme of public works. By 1933, about 59,000 poor whites were employed in various relief measures – irrigation schemes, road and dam building, but especially employment on the railways and in the new state-owned iron and steel giant, ISCOR. By 1939, the central government employed 98,000 white workers, over half of whom were on relief works. In the short term, concludes Iraj Abedian, it was the systematic and elaborate public works programme that most rapidly eliminated white poverty.[24] The third thrust of Pact and Fusion policies saw the sustained expansion of government services to white families. By the late 1930s, legislation had created the basis of a remarkable welfare state for whites. There was also a massive drive to improve the standards of white schooling. It was this investment in human capital that in the longer term eradicated white poverty.

This is not to suggest that any government today could simply scale up and replicate that package of policies to address the poor black problem. But there may be some lessons. Systematic job creation on infrastructure projects should surely play a role. 'There is near unanimous agreement that debt-financed spending on infrastructure raises productivity, enhances competitiveness and can have strong multiplier effects', write Gilad Isaacs and Ben Fine, citing a 2014 IMF finding.[25] And, indeed, surely this was observable during the growth spurt that accompanied the building of the Gautrain and World Cup stadiums? Yet current ANC policy has opted for something much more cautious: the NDP appears to have moved completely away from earlier policy packages that saw a central role for labour-intensive infrastructure projects in job creation.[26]

Redistribution through welfare and the 'social wage'
As we have seen, the ANC government has a substantial record of redistribution and a modest record of poverty alleviation, especially through social grants. State spending on social welfare – together with that on housing, health care, education and municipal services – constitutes the 'social wage'. There are many today

who ask whether such spending is by now more or less at its limit. An alternative question is: what would the trade-off be if it were expanded? As argued in the previous chapter, there is a coherent case to be made for a BIG as a logical extension of the cash transfers already in place. A BIG confronts realities that existing social security provisions fail to do, including the fiction that every work-seeker, sooner or later, will find a decent job. It promises to yield the same sort of economic and developmental benefits that other cash transfers have been shown to achieve.[27] There are also proposals for a basic income grant to the youth population (16–34), allowing young unemployed people access to financial assets that can be leveraged.[28] Whether a BIG went to all, or to the youth population, it would benefit the structurally unemployed, currently largely excluded from the welfare net. It is important to note that either of these could be funded through increases in inheritance tax, capital gains tax and corporation taxes. Because income distribution is so unequal in South Africa, a relatively small reduction in the income of the rich would make a relatively large difference to incomes of the poor.

Addressing skill shortages

There is a huge surplus of unskilled labour *and* a shortage of skilled labour in South Africa. Significant increases in the skills levels of the unskilled would make a substantial impact on unemployment – and government knows this. So there has been a torrent of legislation, projects and plans: the Skills Development Act, and the Skills Education Training Authorities (SETAs) it created; the Skills Development Levies Act; the National Skills Development Strategy; the Human Resource Development Strategy; the National Skills Fund – and so on. Yet all this effort has yielded meagre results. There are any number of reasons for this, including the poor performance of the SETAs; but a central failure resides in the fact that two decades of democracy have done so little to improve a drastically deficient school system. For those in power, this represents one of their greatest failures; for those affected, it is a tragedy.

Pro-poor land reform

At first glance, it might seem obvious that land reform could be a policy implement that would directly address the grinding poverty in the former homelands. These are still zones of vulnerability, doing significantly worse than the rest of South Africa on a whole range of indicators of deprivation. In fact, the disappointing outcomes of land reform and rural development are all too familiar. The willing-buyer-willing-seller model tends only to release poorer arable land; the grip on local affairs by chiefs and 'traditional rulers' is a massive impediment to real reform; smallholders created by redistributed land lack skills, capital, livestock; the market in agricultural products is dominated by agri-business – and so on.

Ruth Hall suggests some straightforward policy shifts: mechanisms to ring-fence resources for the poor; redistribution rooted in participatory and consultative local processes; investment in institutions and settlement patterns that are appropriate for smallholder production; targeted land acquisition rather than purchases through the open market; and providing basic land-use support such as fencing, pumps, tractor services and extension advice. These are not radical proposals, yet they would represent a substantial break with the current mix of market dependence and top-down statism.[29]

All these policy options offer some reduction of poverty. But none can unlock the problem by itself. There is no silver bullet. But to make some combination of these options effective requires social imagination and political will that seem in short supply. As poverty and unemployment are structural in nature, substantially reducing poverty and unemployment requires structural reforms, structural changes. And this is the crux of the very limited impact of the ANC's pro-poor policies since 1994. Persistent poverty is not so much the result of 'not enough' growth, but the product of the wrong kind of growth. There has been economic growth since 1994 – at an annualised rate of about 3% – but it has taken place within an existing growth path. Post-apartheid governments inherited an economy dominated by large corporations, with capital highly concentrated and vertically integrated. But far from attempting any reconfiguration of the political economy, the ANC has entrenched it. Far from reining in or regulating the dominant conglomerates, the ANC deregulated them and authorised capital flight on a massive scale.

The economy continues to be dominated by large corporations; production has become more capital-intensive. Hundreds of thousands of jobs have been shed in mining, agriculture and manufacturing. Unemployment and poverty were part of the apartheid legacy. Of course they were. But their persistence has been partly produced by the nature and course of *post*-apartheid economic policy.[30] The ANC government has failed to address the structural dimensions of poverty and unemployment – not least because the beneficiaries of BEE and boardroom deals have done very well under the existing economic growth path. As Haroon Bhorat and his colleagues pointed out recently, 'No country, to date, has managed to transition out of a middle-income to a high-income status, without the dynamism of a vibrant, labour-intensive manufacturing industry.' Yet in the lexicon of Trevor Manuel, Tito Mboweni, Pravin Gordhan, Cyril Ramaphosa and their colleagues, the language of labour-intensive manufacturing as a driver of growth in jobs is strikingly absent. Instead, one of the biggest drivers of such job creation as has taken place since the mid-1990s has been the expansion of employment in public sector services.[31]

We live at a paradoxical moment. There is a 'nearly

universal agreement that poverty is an important problem ... In policy-making circles, in the public sphere and across almost the entire political spectrum from left to right, South Africans seem to agree that the existence of poverty poses a profound challenge.'[32] And yet this pro-poor consensus has not produced pro-poor outcomes. Perhaps the paradox exists because the consensus on poverty – that it is unacceptable and needs to be eradicated – asks the wrong questions and so comes up with the wrong answers. Tackling poverty decisively is not a technical question of getting the statistics and measurements right. Tackling poverty decisively requires instead changing the social processes and relations that constitute and underpin poverty. Ralph Miliband made this point clearly and forcibly. Looking at poverty, he wrote, we should focus 'first and foremost on the respective strength of conflicting forces operating in society, some making for the persistence of poverty, and others working against its persistence; and the trouble, for the poor, is that the forces operating against them are very much stronger than those working in their favour. What is involved here is not ... the discovery of the right policies, or the creation of the right administrative framework ... The matter goes deeper than that, and concerns the distribution of power in society.'

Ultimately, meeting the challenge of poverty and inequality requires a political solution, not a technical one. In South Africa, this would mean a realignment of political forces that would make a fundamental policy shift possible. It will require a political challenge to an ANC government so deeply implicated in the status quo, and so reluctant to seek structural solutions to structural problems. Such political realignment – let me be clear – is unlikely to be delivered simply through party politics in the narrow sense. It is far more likely to arise from participatory democracy than from representative democracy. It will require the re-mobilisation of the citizenry, pressure from below on politicians, and the deepening of democracy. These, many believe, are desirable in their own right. If they also allow South Africans to tackle poverty and inequality, they are doubly so.

Notes

INTRODUCTION

1 E.G. Malherbe, *Education and the Poor White*, vol. III, Carnegie Commission, pp. xv, xxv; see also pp. 64–7, 156.

2 Rachel Jewkes, 'Intimate partner violence: Causes and prevention', *The Lancet*, 359 (April 2002), 1423–9, p. 1424.

3 Grace Davie, *Poverty Knowledge in South Africa: A Social History of Human Science, 1855–2005* (CUP, 2015), p. 3.

4 Ibid., pp. 14–15.

5 Peter Alcock, *Understanding Poverty*, 3rd edn (Palgrave Macmillan, 2006), pp. 4–5.

6 Ibid., pp. 69–75.

7 Davie, *Poverty Knowledge*, pp. 101, 126, 140.

8 The United Nations convened a World Summit for Social Development, held in Copenhagen in 1995.

9 Diana Wylie, *Starving on a Full Stomach* (University Press of Virginia, 2001), p. 8; see also L. Reynolds, '"Making known" or "counting our children"? Constructing and caring for children in epidemic South Africa', *Medical Anthropology Theory*, 1, 1, (2014), 114–43, p. 140.

10 Jeremy Seekings and Nicoli Nattrass, *Policy, Politics and Poverty in South Africa* (Palgrave Macmillan, 2015), pp. 30–7, discuss some of the complexities of quantitative data and the debates and contested interpretations that have taken place since 1994.

11 Mark Gevisser, *Thabo Mbeki: The Dream Deferred* (Jonathan Ball,

2007), p. 692, quoted in Davie, *Poverty Knowledge*, p. 251. Davie provides a lively account of contested knowledge, pp. 251–78.

12 The concept is closely associated with Neville Alexander, who deployed and reworked the notion for several decades. A recent thoughtful reappraisal of the concept's pertinence is Michael Cloete, 'Neville Alexander: Towards overcoming the legacy of racial capitalism in post-apartheid South Africa', *Transformation*, 86 (2014), 30–47.

13 Charles H. Feinstein, *An Economic History of South Africa* (CUP, 2005), p. 47.

14 Strictly speaking, the ANC only declared a 'war against poverty' in 2008, in President Mbeki's State of the Nation address. I am applying the metaphor to the various 'pro-poor' and 'anti-poverty' efforts from the RDP manifesto of 1994 onwards.

15 David Everatt, 'The undeserving poor: Poverty and the politics of service delivery in the poorest nodes of South Africa', *Politikon*, 35, 3 (2008), 293–319, pp. 294, 305, 308.

CHAPTER 1

1 A good summary of such scholarship is available in Carolyn Hamilton, Bernard Mbenga and Robert Ross (eds.), *The Cambridge History of South Africa, vol. 1, From Early Times to 1885* (CUP, 2010).

2 Quoted in John Iliffe, *The African Poor: A History* (CUP, 1987), p. 3.

3 Iliffe, *The African Poor*, p. 2.

4 Ibid., pp. 4–6.

5 Jeff Peires, *The House of Phalo: A History of the Xhosa People* (Ravan, 1981), p. 77.

6 Richard Elphick, *Khoikhoi and the Founding of White South Africa* (Ravan, 1985), p. 37; Richard Elphick and V.C. Malherbe, 'The Khoisan to 1828', in Richard Elphick and Hermann Giliomee (eds.), *The Shaping of South African Society, 1652–1840* (Maskew Miller Longman, 1989), pp. 6–7.

7 Elphick, *Khoikhoi*, p. 94; Iliffe, *The African Poor*, p. 70.

8 Paragraph based on John Wright, 'Turbulent times: Political transformations in the north and east, 1760s–1830s', in Hamilton, Mbenga and Ross, *Cambridge History of South Africa, 1*.

9 Paragraph based on Peter Delius, *The Land Belongs to Us* (Ravan, 1983), pp. 50–2; Norman Etherington, *The Great Treks: The Transformation of Southern Africa 1815–1854* (Pearson, 2001),

pp. 14–15; Iliffe, *The African Poor*, pp. 74–81; Wright, 'Turbulent times', pp. 218, 223, 229–30, quotation p. 230.

10 Leonard Guelke, 'Freehold farmers and frontier settlers, 1657–1780', in Elphick and Giliomee, *The Shaping of South African Society*, p. 67.

11 May Katzen, 'White settlers and the origins of a new society', in Monica Wilson and Leonard Thompson (eds.), *The Oxford History of South Africa, vol. 1* (OUP, 1969), p. 232; for a full-blown version of the myth of Boer egalitarianism, see Sheila Patterson, *The Last Trek: A Study of the Boer People and the Afrikaner Nation* (Routledge Kegan Paul, 1957).

12 Paragraph based on Susan Newton-King, *Masters and Servants on the Cape Eastern Frontier 1760–1803* (CUP, 1999), pp. 18–24.

13 P.J. van der Merwe, *The Migrant Farmer in the History of the Cape Colony, 1657–1842*, transl. by R. Beck (Ohio University Press, 1995, orig. publ. in Afrikaans, 1938), pp. 162–3; Newton-King, *Masters and Servants*, pp. 196–200, 204.

14 Iliffe, *The African Poor*, p. 98.

15 Newton-King, *Masters and Servants*, pp. 207, 41, 44, 114–17.

16 Martin Legassick and Robert Ross, 'From slave economy to settler capitalism, 1800–1854', in Hamilton, Mbenga and Ross, *Cambridge History of South Africa, I*, p. 303.

17 Paragraph based on Martin Legassick, *The Struggle for the Eastern Cape, 1800–1854* (KMM, 2010), pp. 88–96 and Clifton Crais, *Poverty, War and Violence in South Africa* (CUP, 2011), pp. 39–54; quotations from Crais, pp. 39, 43, 53.

18 Paragraph based on Lance van Sittert, 'Children for ewes: Child indenture in the post-emancipation Great Karoo c1856–1909', *JSAS*, 42, 4 (2016), 743–62.

19 Paragraph based on Norman Etherington, Patrick Harries and Bernard Mbenga, 'From colonial hegemonies to imperial conquest, 1840–1880', in Hamilton, Mbenga and Ross, *Cambridge History of South Africa, I*, pp. 340–9; Peter Delius and Stanley Trapido, '*Inboekselings* and *Oorlams*: The creation and transformation of a servile class', *JSAS*, 8, 2 (1982), quotation p. 214.

CHAPTER 2

1 This and preceding paragraph draw from Colin Bundy, 'Vagabond Hollanders and runaway Englishmen: White poverty in the Cape before Poor Whiteism', in W. Beinart, P. Delius and S. Trapido

   (eds.), *Putting a Plough to the Ground* (Ravan, 1986), pp. 107–8, 110–13.

2 Paragraph based on Nigel Worden, Elizabeth van Heyningen and Vivian Bickford-Smith, *Cape Town: The Making of a City* (David Philip, 1998), pp. 12–21, 182, 184.

3 Paragraph based on Bundy, 'Vagabond Hollanders', p. 116.

4 Ibid., especially pp. 103–4, 119–23.

5 Vivian Bickford-Smith, *Ethnic Pride and Racial Prejudice in Victorian Cape Town* (CUP, 1995), pp. 91–100, 116–18.

6 Sarah E. Duff, *Changing Childhoods in the Cape Colony: Dutch Reformed Church Evangelicism and Colonial Childhood, 1860–1895* (Palgrave Macmillan, 2015), pp. 28, 125.

7 Gareth Stedman-Jones, *Outcast London* (OUP, 1971), p. 327.

8 Jennifer Muirhead and Sandra Swart, 'The whites of the child? Race and class in the politics of child welfare in Cape Town, c1900–1924', *Journal of the History of Childhood and Youth*, 8, 2 (Spring 2015), 229–53, p. 235.

9 Timothy Keegan, *Rural Transformations in Industrializing South Africa* (Ravan, 1986), p. 22, cited in Lis Lange, *White, Poor and Angry: White Working Class Families in Johannesburg* (Ashgate, 2003), p. 24.

10 Lange, *White, Poor and Angry*, pp. 81–2, 149.

11 Muirhead and Swart, 'The whites of the child?', p. 234.

12 Lange, *White, Poor and Angry*, p. 83.

13 Ibid., pp. 152–3.

14 Davie, *Poverty Knowledge in South Africa*, p. 41.

15 Ernest G. Malherbe, *Never a Dull Moment* (Howard Timmins, 1981), p. 119, quoted in Hermann Giliomee, *The Afrikaners: Biography of a People* (Hurst, 2004), p. 346.

16 Davie, *Poverty Knowledge in South Africa*, p, 82. See also C.J. Groenewald, 'The methodology of poverty research in South Africa: The case of the first Carnegie investigation 1929–1932', *Social Dynamics*, 13, 2 (1987), 60–74.

17 Paragraph based on Feinstein, *Economic History*, pp. 86–8; Philip Bonner, 'South African culture and society 1910–1948', in Robert Ross, Anne Kelk Mager and Bill Nasson (eds.), *Cambridge History of South Africa, vol. 2, 1885–1994* (CUP, 2011), p. 298; Nicoli Nattrass and Jeremy Seekings, 'The economy and poverty in the twentieth century', in Ross, Mager and Nasson, *Cambridge History*, 2, pp. 527–32.

18 Paragraph based on Iraj Abedian, Steffen Schneier and Barry Standish, 'The role of public works programmes in combating poverty in South Africa', Carnegie Conference, Post-conference series no. 10 (November 1985), pp. 16–22.

19 Susan Parnell, 'Slums, segregation and poor whites in Johannesburg, 1920–34', in Robert Morrell (ed.), *White but Poor: Essays on the History of Poor Whites in Southern Africa 1880–1940* (Unisa Press, 1992), pp. 126–9, quotation p. 128.

20 Jeremy Seekings, '"Not a single white person should be allowed to go under": Swart gevaar and the origins of South Africa's welfare state', *Journal of African History*, 48, 3 (2007), p. 382.

21 Paragraph based on Seekings, '"Not a single white person"', pp. 376, 379; Andreas Sagner, 'Ageing and social policy in South Africa: Historical perspectives with particular reference to the Eastern Cape', *JSAS*, 26, 3 (2000), p. 529; James Ferguson, *Give a Man a Fish: Reflections on the New Politics of Distribution* (Duke University Press, 2015), p. 73.

22 Jeremy Seekings, 'The Carnegie Commission and the backlash against welfare state-building in South Africa, 1931–1937', *JSAS*, 34, 3 (2008), pp. 515–16.

23 Feinstein, *Economic History*, p. 88; Giliomee, *The Afrikaners*, p. 336; Nattrass and Seekings, 'The economy and poverty', p. 532.

CHAPTER 3

1 See Paul la Hausse, 'The struggle for the city: Alcohol, the Ematsheni and popular culture in Durban, 1902–1936', in Paul Maylam and Iain Edwards (eds.), *The People's City: African Life in Twentieth-Century Durban* (University of Natal Press, 1996), pp. 44–8.

2 David Duncan, *The Mills of God: The State and African Labour in South Africa 1919–1948* (Wits University Press, 1995), pp. 91, 93.

3 William Beinart, *Twentieth Century South Africa*, 2nd edn (OUP, 2001), p. 134.

4 Ibid., p. 201.

5 William M. Macmillan, *Complex South Africa: An Economic Foot-note to History* (Faber & Faber, 1930), pp. 147, 160, 177–8, 182, 185.

6 Ibid., pp. 54, 121, 137, 138, 38–9, *et passim*.

7 Jeremy Krikler, 'William Macmillan and the working class', in Hugh Macmillan and Shula Marks (eds.), *Africa and Empire: W.M. Macmillan, Historian and Social Critic* (Gower, 1989), p. 54;

William Beinart, 'W.M. Macmillan's analysis of agrarian change and African rural communities', in Macmillan and Marks, *Africa and Empire*, p. 168.

8 Charles Simkins, 'Agricultural production in the African reserves of South Africa, 1918–1969', *JSAS*, 7, 2 (1980), 256–83, pp. 262–4, 270–1.

9 Feinstein, *Economic History*, pp. 70–2.

10 Iliffe, *The African Poor*, p. 126.

11 Wylie, *Starving on a Full Stomach*, p. 60; and see her examination of three such famines in 1912, 1927 and 1946, pp. 61–90.

12 Alan Jeeves, *Migrant Labour in South Africa's Mining Economy* (Witwatersrand University Press, 1985), p. 264.

13 Paragraph based on Colin Bundy, *The Rise and Fall of a South African Peasantry*, 2nd edn (James Currey, 1988), pp. 225–6.

14 Alan Jeeves and Jonathan Crush, 'Introduction' in Jeeves and Crush (eds.), *White Farms, Black Labor: The State and Agrarian Change in Southern Africa, 1910–1950* (Heinemann and James Currey, 1997), p. 5.

15 Helen Bradford, *A Taste of Freedom: The ICU in Rural South Africa, 1924–1930* (Yale University Press, 1987), p. 36.

16 Jeeves and Crush, 'Introduction', p. 26.

17 Duncan, *Mills of God*, p. 137.

18 Doreen Atkinson, *Going for Broke: The Fate of Farm Workers in Arid South Africa* (HSRC Press, 2007), p. 38.

19 Helen Bradford, 'Getting away with murder: "Mealie kings", the state and foreigners in the Eastern Transvaal, c.1918–1950', in P. Bonner, P. Delius and D. Posel (eds.), *Apartheid's Genesis 1935–1962* (Ravan Press, 1993), p. 106.

20 Francis Wilson, 'Farming 1866–1966', in Monica Wilson and Leonard Thompson (eds.), *The Oxford History of South Africa, vol. 2* (OUP, 1971), pp. 146–7.

21 In 1936, the Harvard sociologist James Ford defined a slum in lastingly influential terms as 'a residential area in which the housing is so deteriorated, so substandard or so unwholesome as to be a menace to the health, safety, morality or welfare of the occupants'.

22 Cited in Feinstein, *Economic History*, p. 71.

23 Iliffe, *The African Poor*, p. 128.

24 Quotations from Elleke Boehmer, *Nelson Mandela: A Very Short Introduction* (OUP, 2008), p. 112; David Coplan, *In Township*

Tonight! South Africa's Black City Music and Theatre (Ravan Press, 1985), p. 144. A good outline history of the earlier years is provided by André Proctor, 'Class struggle, segregation and the city: A history of Sophiatown 1905–1940', in Belinda Bozzoli (ed.), *Labour, Townships and Protest* (Ravan Press, 1979). Nostalgic accounts include Can Themba, 'Requiem for Sophiatown', *Africa South*, 3, 3 (1958) and Bloke Modisane, *Blame Me on History* (Thames & Hudson, 1963); see also the evocation of Sophiatown by Trevor Huddleston, *Naught for Your Comfort* (Collins, 1956), pp. 121–34.

25 Leslie Bank, *Home Spaces, Street Styles: Contesting Power and Identity in a South African City* (Pluto, 2011), pp. 37, 41–2.

26 Deborah Posel, 'The apartheid project, 1948–1970', in Ross, Mager and Nasson, *Cambridge History of South Africa, 2*, p. 323.

27 Peter Wilkinson, 'Providing "adequate shelter": The South African state and the "resolution" of the African urban housing crisis', in Doug Hindson (ed.), *Working Papers in Southern African Studies, vol. 3* (Ravan, 1983), p. 78.

28 For detailed analysis of these figures, with gender and age breakdown, see Michael P. Proctor, 'Capital, state and the African population of Johannesburg, 1921–1980', in Dennis Cordell and Joel Gregory (eds.), *African Populations and Capitalism: Historical Perspectives* (University of Wisconsin Press, 1987), pp. 255ff.

29 Bill Freund, *The African City: A History* (CUP, 2007), p. 111.

30 Ellen Hellman, *Rooiyard: A Sociological Survey of an Urban Native Slum Yard* (OUP, 1948).

31 Ibid., pp. 7–8. 10, 11–13, 37–8; Iliffe, *The African Poor*, p. 129.

32 Belinda Bozzoli, *Theatres of Struggle and the End of Apartheid* (Edinburgh University Press, 2004), pp. 22–8, 42–7, quotations pp. 23, 25.

33 Nelson Mandela, *Long Walk to Freedom* (Macdonald Purnell, 1994), pp. 65, 71–3.

34 Paragraph based on Bonner, 'South African society and culture 1910–1948', pp. 189–90; Bank, *Home Spaces*, pp. 21–2; William Beinart and Colin Bundy, 'The union, the nation and the talking crow: Ideology and tactics of the Independent ICU in East London', in Beinart and Bundy, *Hidden Struggles in Rural South Africa* (James Currey, 1987), p. 274.

35 Paragraph based on Bonner, 'South African society and culture', pp. 287–8; Paul Maylam, 'Introduction', in Maylam and Edwards,

The People's City, pp. 15–20, quotation p. 19.

36 Paragraph based on Davie, *Poverty Knowledge in South Africa*, pp. 106–9, 113–15; Vivian Bickford-Smith, Elizabeth van Heyningen and Nigel Worden, *Cape Town in the Twentieth Century* (David Philip, 1999), pp. 103–8, quotations pp. 103, 107.

CHAPTER 4

1 Beinart, *Twentieth Century South Africa*, p. 144.

2 Deborah Posel, *The Making of Apartheid 1948–1961* (OUP, 1991), p. 1.

3 This formulation based on Posel, 'The apartheid project', p. 341.

4 Quoted in William Minter, *King Solomon's Mines Revisited* (Basic Books, 1986), p. 75.

5 Feinstein, *Economic History*, pp. 146–8.

6 Ibid., p. 150.

7 Paragraph based on Beinart, *Twentieth Century South Africa*, pp. 125–6; for proportion of females in Johannesburg African population, see Proctor, 'Capital, state and the African population of Johannesburg, 1921–1980', p. 255.

8 Beinart, *Twentieth Century South Africa*, pp. 129–32; Noor Nieftagodien, 'Popular movements, contentious spaces and the ANC, 1943–1956', in Arianna Lissoni, Jon Soske, Natasha Erlank, Noor Nieftagodien and Omar Badsha (eds.), *One Hundred Years of the ANC: Debating Liberation Histories Today* (Wits University Press, 2012), pp. 139–41.

9 Philip Bonner, 'The politics of black squatter movements on the Rand, 1944–1953', in Joshua Brown, Patrick Manning, Karin Shapiro and Jon Wiener (eds.), *History from South Africa: Alternative Visions and Practices* (Temple University Press, 1991), 59–81, p. 63; Nieftagodien, 'Popular movements', p. 141.

10 Nieftagodien, 'Popular movements', pp. 140–1; Dhiru Soni, 'The apartheid state and black housing struggles', in David Smith (ed.), *The Apartheid City and Beyond* (Routledge, 1992), 39–52, p. 41; Bonner, 'Politics of black squatter movements', p. 65.

11 Paul Maylam, 'Explaining the apartheid city', *JSAS*, 21, 1 (1995), 19–38, p. 35.

12 Wilkinson, 'Providing "adequate shelter"', p. 83.

13 Paragraph based on Sue Parnell and Alan Mabin, 'Rethinking urban South Africa', *JSAS*, 21, 1 (1995), 39–62, pp. 53–9; Wilkinson, 'Providing "adequate shelter"'; Derek Japha, 'The

social programme of the South African Modern Movement', in Hilton Judin and Ivan Vladislavić, *Blank: Architecture, Apartheid and After* (David Philip, 1999), pp. 423–38. Verwoerd quotations from Nieftagodien, 'Popular movements', p. 153 and Japha, 'The social programme', p. 432.

14 Bank, *Home Spaces, Street Styles*, p. 69.

15 Nieftagodien, 'Popular movements', p. 154.

16 David Dewar, 'Urban poverty and city development: Some perspectives and guidelines', Carnegie Conference Paper no. 163 (1984), pp. 1, 8, 21.

17 Jacob Dlamini, *Native Nostalgia* (Jacana, 2009).

18 Freund, *The African City*, p. 123.

19 John Western, *Outcast Cape Town* (Human & Rousseau, 1981), quotations from Van der Ross and Theron in Erika Theron, 'Foreword', p. xi; by Western, pp. 273–4.

20 Roger Southall, *The New Black Middle Class in South Africa* (James Currey, 2016), pp. 32–7; Owen Crankshaw, *Race, Class and the Changing Division of Labour under Apartheid* (Routledge, 1997).

21 Freund, *The African City*, p. 126.

CHAPTER 5

1 Paragraph based on Nattrass and Seekings, 'The economy and poverty', pp. 559–60, and Feinstein, *Economic History*; the quotation is from the latter, p. 194.

2 See papers presented to the Carnegie Conference, UCT, 1983, especially papers 43–50 (Transkei), 53–9 (KwaZulu), 60–71 (Lehurutshe, Bophuthatswana, Venda, Lebowa, Gazankulu, Namaqualand).

3 Francis Wilson and Mamphela Ramphele, *Uprooting Poverty* (David Philip, 1989), pp. 39–41, 69–72; Nattrass and Seekings, 'The economy and poverty', pp. 559–60.

4 Posel, 'The apartheid project', pp. 336, 342.

5 Two classic studies of the process are Cosmas Desmond, *The Discarded People: An Account of African Resettlement in South Africa* (Penguin, 1971) and Laurine Platzky and Cherryl Walker, *The Surplus People: Forced Removals in South Africa* (Ravan, 1985).

6 Desmond, *The Discarded People*, p. 1.

7 Platzky and Walker, *The Surplus People*, pp. 330–1. Dimbaza's notoriety is due to the 1975 documentary film *Last Grave at Dimbaza*.

8   These definitions are from General Circular 2 of 1982, quoted in Platzky and Walker, *The Surplus People*, pp. 331–2.

9   Colin Murray, 'Displaced urbanisation' in John Lonsdale (ed.), *South Africa in Question* (University of Cambridge African Studies Centre, 1988), pp. 11, 116.

10 Joseph Lelyveld, *Move Your Shadow* (Jonathan Ball, 1986), p. 125.

11 Colin Bundy, 'Casting a long historical shadow: The Natives Land Act of 1913 and its legacy', in *Umhlaba, 1913–2013: Images from the Exhibition Commemorating the Centenary of the Natives Land Act* (Plaas, UWC, 2015); Michael de Klerk, 'Seasons that will never return: The impact of farm mechanisation on employment, incomes and population distribution in the Western Transvaal', *JSAS*, 11, 1 (1984), pp. 88, 94; Posel, 'The apartheid project', p. 339.

12 Nattrass and Seekings, 'The economy and poverty', p. 557.

13 Ibid; Jeremy Seekings and Nicoli Nattrass, *Class, Race and Inequality in South Africa* (Yale, 2005); Feinstein, *Economic History*.

14 Colin Murray, 'Structural unemployment, small towns and agrarian change in South Africa', *African Affairs*, 94 (1995), 5–22, p. 6. (Murray's article focused on the Free State but is equally true for other regions.)

15 This and the preceding paragraph are based on Seekings and Nattrass, *Class, Race and Inequality*, pp. 173–81; Nattrass and Seekings, 'The economy and poverty', pp. 555–7, 560–8; Feinstein, *Economic History*, pp. 230–40, table based on figure 10.5, p. 239; quotation p. 238.

16 Tom Lodge, 'Resistance and reform, 1973–1994', in Ross, Mager and Nasson, *Cambridge History of South Africa, 2*, 409–91, p. 446.

17 Doug Hindson, 'The apartheid city: Construction, decline and reconstruction', p. 78; accessed at horizon.document.ird.fr/excl-doc/pleines_textes/divers11-10/010005820.pdf .

18 Philip Bonner and Lauren Segal, *Soweto: A History* (Maskew Miller Longman, 1998), pp. 134–6.

19 Owen Crankshaw and Susan Parnell, 'Interpreting the 1994 township landscape', in Juden and Vladislavić, *Blank*, 439–43, p. 441.

20 Maylam, 'Introduction', pp. 24–5; Bank, *Home Spaces, Street Style*, pp. 92–3; Catherine Besteman, *Transforming Cape Town* (University of California Press, 2008), p. 48; Grant Saff, *Changing Cape Town* (University Press of America, 1998), pp. 89–90.

CHAPTER 6

1 Seekings and Nattrass, *Policy, Politics and Poverty*, p. 160.

2 On the 1940s see Bill Freund, 'The South African developmental state of the 1940s', *Transformation*, 81/2 (2013); Deborah Posel, 'The case for a welfare state: Poverty and the politics of the urban African family in the 1930s and 1940s', in Saul Dubow and Alan Jeeves (eds.), *South Africa's 1940s: Worlds of Possibility* (Double Storey, 2005). On the NHS, see Robert van Niekerk, 'Historical roots of a national health system in South Africa', in Greg Ruiters and Robert van Niekerk (eds.), *Universal Health Care in South Africa* (UKZN Press, 2012), pp. 41, 51.

3 Jeremy Seekings, 'Visions, hopes and views about the future: The radical moment of South African welfare reform', in Dubow and Jeeves, *South Africa's 1940s*, p. 44. (William Beveridge chaired the committee which in 1942 produced a report on Social Insurance and Allied Services – often called the 'Beveridge Report' – a key step towards the post-war welfare state in the UK.)

4 Posel, 'The case for a welfare state', p. 66.

5 Iliffe, *The African Poor*, p. 142.

6 This and preceding paragraph based on Seekings and Nattrass, *Class, Race and Inequality*, pp. 147–54, 356, 360; Hein Marais, *South Africa Pushed to the Limit* (Zed, 2011), p. 239.

7 For a vivid sense of this process, see the proceedings of the symposium on 'The role of research in transforming South Africa' in *Transformation*, special issue 18/19 (1992).

8 Francie Lund, *Changing Social Policy: The Child Support Grant in South Africa* (HSRC Press, 2008), pp. 4–9, quotation p. 6; and see her 'A race against time: Managing change in the new South Africa', *Soundings*, 4 (1996), pp. 121–34.

9 Marais, *South Africa Pushed to the Limit*, p. 241.

10 See M. de Paoli, E.A. Mills and A.B. Grønningsaeter, 'The ARV roll out and the disability grant: A South African dilemma?', *Journal of the International AIDS Society*, 15, 6 (2012); and Nicoli Nattrass, 'Disability and welfare in South Africa's era of unemployment and AIDS', in S. Buhlungu, John Daniel, Roger Southall and Jessica Lutchman (eds.), *State of the Nation: South Africa 2007* (HSRC Press, 2007).

11 Figure 1 from Seekings and Nattrass, *Policy, Politics and Poverty*, p. 137.

12 Ferguson, *Give a Man a Fish*, pp. 78–9.

13 Keith Breckenridge, *Biometric State: The Global Politics of Identification and Surveillance in South Africa: 1850 to the Present* (CUP, 2014).

14 This and preceding paragraph based on Breckenridge, *Biometric State*, pp. 137, 181–7.

15 Kevin Donovan, 'The biometric imaginary: Bureaucratic technopolitics in post-apartheid welfare', *JSAS*, 41, 4 (2015), 815–33, pp. 819–20, 832.

16 Ibid., pp. 832–3; Breckenridge, *Biometric State*, p. 214.

17 Paragraph based on Seekings and Nattrass, *Policy, Politics and Poverty*, pp. 136–7, 139–40, 159.

18 Ferguson, *Give a Man a Fish*, pp. 7–8, 14–19, 102–17, 136–40; Seekings and Nattrass, *Policy, Politics and Poverty*, pp. 136–41, 147–50; D. Neves, M. Samson, I. van Niekerk, S. Hlatshwayo and A. du Toit, 'The use and effectiveness of social grants in South Africa' (Finmark Trust, 2009).

19 Seekings and Nattrass, *Policy, Politics and Poverty*, pp. 140–1.

20 Jonny Steinberg, 'Idea of jobs for all blinds us to need for welfare', *Business Day*, 26 July 2013.

21 Erik Bahre, 'Liberation and redistribution: Social grants, commercial insurance and religious riches in South Africa', *Comparative Studies in Society and History*, 53, 2 (2011), pp. 381–2.

22 S. Jehoma, former DDG in Department, quoted in G. Wright, M. Noble, P. Ntshongwana, D. Neves and H. Barnes, 'The role of social security in respecting and protecting the dignity of lone mothers in South Africa: Final report' (CASASP, 2014), p. 131.

23 Quoted in Robert van Niekerk, 'Social policy, social citizenship and the historical idea of a social democratic welfare state in South Africa', *Transformation*, 81/2 (2013), p. 116.

24 Jeremy Seekings and Heidi Matisonn, 'South Africa: The continuing politics of basic income', in Matthew Murray and Carole Pateman (eds.), *Basic Income Worldwide: Horizons of Reform* (Palgrave Macmillan, 2012), p. 132.

25 See Charles Meth, 'Ideology and social policy: "Handouts" and the spectre of "dependency"', *Transformation*, 56 (2004), p. 15; Mbeki quoted in Everatt, 'The undeserving poor', pp. 299, 302, 311.

26 Franco Barchiesi, 'South African debates on the Big Income Grant: Wage labour and the post-apartheid social policy', *JSAS*, 33, 3 (2007), p. 568; Van Niekerk, 'Social policy, social citizenship', p. 116; Everatt, 'The undeserving poor', p. 305.

27 Paragraph based on Barchiesi, 'South African debates', pp. 571–4.

28 Heidi Matisonn and Jeremy Seekings, 'The politics of a basic income grant in South Africa, 1996–2002', in Guy Standing and Michael Sansom, *A Basic Income Grant for South Africa* (UCT Press, 2003), p. 63; Zola Skweyiya, 'Building an inclusive, comprehensive and non-discriminatory social welfare system in post-apartheid South Africa', inaugural Skweyiya Lecture, Oxford, May 2011; text available: https://www.spi.ox.ac.uk/fileadmin/documents/PDF/ZS_final_version_oxford_lecture_as_delivered_on_17_May_2011_1700.pdf; Seekings and Matisonn, 'South Africa: The continuing politics of basic income', p. 140.

29 Seekings and Nattrass, *Policy, Politics and Poverty*, p. 161.

30 Ferguson, *Give a Man a Fish*, p. 2.

31 James Ferguson, 'The uses of neoliberalism', *Antipode*, 41 (2010), p. 174.

32 Paragraph draws on Ferguson, *Give a Man a Fish*, pp. 29–30, 79–84.

33 Adam Whitworth and Michael Noble, 'A safety net without holes: An argument for a comprehensive income security system for South Africa', *Journal of Human Development*, 9, 2 (2008), p. 252.

34 Jonny Steinberg, 'Grants encourage liberation, not dependence', *Business Day*, 23 August 2013.

35 Ferguson, *Give a Man a Fish*, pp. 56–7.

36 Marais, *South Africa Pushed to the Limit*, p. 250.

37 Everatt, 'The undeserving poor', p. 301.

CHAPTER 7

1 Murray Leibbrandt, Ingrid Woolard, Arden Finn and Jonathan Argent, 'Trends in South African income distribution and poverty since the fall of apartheid', *OECD Social, Employment and Migration Working Papers, no. 101* (OECD Publishing, 2010), p. 21.

2 Specifically, those percentages fell below a poverty line of R322 per month at 2000 rand values: cited in Johannes Hoogeveen and Berk Özler, 'Not separate, not equal: Poverty and inequality in post-apartheid South Africa', in Haroon Bhorat and Ravi Kanbur (eds.), *Poverty and Policy in Post-Apartheid South Africa* (HSRC Press, 2006), p. 59.

3 Leibbrandt, Woolard, Finn and Argent, 'Trends', p. 17.

4 David Fryer, '"State of the art" or dismal science? The economic debate in South Africa since 1994', *Arts and Humanities in Higher Education*, 51, 1 (2016), 122–39, pp. 125–6.

5 Terry Bell, quoted in Brij Maharaj, Ashwin Desai and Patrick Bond, 'Introduction: Poverty eradication as the Holy Grail', in Maharaj, Desai and Bond (eds.), *Zuma's Own Goal: Losing South Africa's War on Poverty* (Africa World Press, 2011), pp. 18–19.

6 The three are (in order of publication) Bhorat and Kanbur, *Poverty and Policy*; Leibbrandt, Woolard, Finn and Argent, 'Trends'; Seekings and Nattrass, *Policy, Politics and Poverty*.

7 Hoogeveen and Özler, 'Not separate, not equal', pp. 59, 61–2; Haroon Bhorat and Ravi Kanbur, 'Poverty and well-being in post-*apartheid* South Africa', in Bhorat and Kanbur, *Poverty and Policy*, p. 2; Leibbrandt, Woolard, Finn and Argent, 'Trends', p. 14; Seekings and Nattrass, *Policy, Politics and Poverty*, p. 37.

8 Seekings and Nattrass, *Policy, Politics and Poverty*, p. 183; Bhorat and Kanbur, 'Poverty and well-being', p. 7; Leibbrandt, Woolard, Finn and Argent, 'Trends', pp. 42, 44.

9 Ivan Turok and Jackie Borel-Saladin, 'Continuity, change and conflict in South African cities', in Thenjiwe Meyiwa, Muxe Nkondo, Margaret Chitiga-Mabugu, Moses Sithole and Francis Nyamnjoh (eds.), *State of the Nation 2014* (HSRC Press, 2014), p. 183; Bhorat and Kanbur, 'Poverty and well-being', p. 7.

10 Leibbrandt, Woolard, Finn and Argent, 'Trends', p. 32.

11 Ibid., p. 26.

12 Murray Leibbrandt, Eva Wegner and Arden Finn, 'The policies for reducing income inequality and poverty in South Africa', SALDRU Working Paper 64 (2011).

13 Paragraph draws on Susan Booysen, *Dominance and Decline: The ANC in the Time of Zuma* (Wits University Press, 2015), pp. 98, 152–3, 270.

14 Paragraph quotes from Mike Rogan and John Reynolds, 'How high unemployment has eclipsed the plight of South Africa's working poor', *Mail & Guardian*, 12 August 2015; Carol Paton, 'Study on how to lift workers out of poverty', *Business Day*, 26 August 2015; Gilad Isaacs, 'South Africa's 5-million working poor', *Daily Maverick*, 26 August 2015.

15 Leibbrandt, Woolard, Finn and Argent, 'Trends', pp. 9, 15, 37.

16 Turok and Borel-Saladin, 'Continuity, change and conflict', pp. 186–8.

17 Bank, *Home Spaces, Street Styles*, pp. 211, 223; Anton Harber, *Diepsloot* (Jonathan Ball, 2011), p. 3.

18 Harber, *Diepsloot*, p. 224.

19 Ibid., pp. 43, 101, 170, 120 *et passim*.

20 Andries du Toit and David Neves, 'The government of poverty and the arts of survival: Mobile and recombinant strategies at the margins of the South African economy', *Journal of Peasant Studies*, 41, 5 (2014); quotations at p. 12.

21 Paragraph based on Seekings and Nattrass, *Policy, Politics and Poverty*, pp. 100–4.

22 Paragraph draws on Gilad Isaacs and Ben Fine, 'The national minimum wage debate: Looking beyond a narrow focus on labour markets', *Econ3x3*, March 2015, and Neil Coleman, 'South Africa needs serious interventions to fix extreme inequality', *Daily Maverick*, 6 October 2015.

23 Frederick Fourie, 'Reducing unemployment: Waiting for high growth? Waiting for Godot?', *Econ3x3*, March 2013.

24 Paragraph based on Abedian, Schneier and Standish, 'The role of public works programmes in combating poverty in South Africa', pp. 16–22.

25 Isaacs and Fine, 'The national minimum wage debate'.

26 Frederick Fourie, 'The NDP on unemployment: On consistency, coherence and comprehensiveness', *REDI3x3*, Working Paper 7 (May 2015).

27 Hein Marais, '7 reasons why a universal income makes sense in middle-income countries', *Global Labour Column* (Corporate Strategy and Industrial Development, University of the Witwatersrand), 70 (September 2011).

28 Lauren Graham, 'Just give them the money? Building youth assets as an option to enhance youth outcomes', in Jan Hofmeyr (ed.), *Transformation Audit 2012: The Youth Dividend: Unlocking the Potential of Young South Africans* (Institute of Justice and Reconciliation, 2012).

29 Ruth Hall, 'Who, what, where, how, why? The many disagreements about land redistribution in South Africa', in B. Cousins and C. Walker (eds.), *Land Divided, Land Restored* (Jacana, 2015).

30 This and the preceding paragraph draw upon two papers by Andries du Toit: 'The trouble with poverty: Reflections on South Africa's post-apartheid anti-poverty consensus', PLAAS Working Paper 22 (PLAAS, UWC, 2012) and 'The government of poverty and the arts of survival', Paper prepared for *Towards Carnegie 3: Conference on Strategies to Overcome Poverty and Inequality* (UCT,

2012); some of the material is reworked in Du Toit and Neves, 'The government of poverty'.

31 Haroon Bhorat, Karmen Naidoo, Morné Oosthuizen and Kavisha Pillay, 'Demographic, employment and wage trends in South Africa', WIDER Working Paper 2015/141 (December 2015); quotation p. 3, see also pp. 8–10.

32 Du Toit, 'The trouble with poverty', p. 1.

Acknowledgements

It is a pleasure to thank those who have aided, encouraged or endured my attempts to think and write about poverty in South Africa. The chapters that follow had a preliminary airing as a Summer School course at the University of Cape Town. I am grateful to Medee Rall and her colleagues who accepted the proposal (with some doubts, they subsequently confessed, whether the topic would attract students!). In fact, just over a hundred people signed up for the course. Their engagement in the topic was expressed in the probing questions they put, but also in the emotional intensity of their responses.

A number of friends and colleagues read or commented on some or all of the chapters. I am especially indebted to Murray Leibbrandt and Pieter le Roux, economists who were generously tolerant of an historian trespassing on their turf. Others who read draft chapters were William Beinart, Eve Bertelsen, Lucie Cluver, Hannah Dawson, Merle Lipton, Michael Noble, Jeff Rudin and Gemma Wright. The range of intellectual and political positions that they brought to the text neatly ensured that virtually all my findings were disputed – which is exactly why one values such assistance. It goes without saying that any remaining flaws are mine. I also benefited through feedback from participants at the Zola Skweyiya Lecture, which I delivered at the invitation of Rebecca Surender, and the South African discussion group convened by Jonny Steinberg.

Finally, this is the fourth volume that I have written for the Jacana pocket series; for all of them I have been fortunate enough to have had the same meticulous, eagle-eyed and enthusiastic editor. It has been a pleasure working with Russell Martin, and it is difficult to imagine Jacana without him.

Index

'Our Plan for the Next Five Years', the sole reference to social welfare was a cautious commitment to 'establish a consensus on our future social security system to make it comprehensive and inclusive'.

Five years on, 2014 saw another election year, and another ANC manifesto: *Together We Move South Africa Forward*. It is longer and much more detailed than the 1994 version – but equally reticent on the issue of social security: it has been dubbed 'remarkably coy about welfare reform'.[1] Towards its end, there are eight sentences on social welfare. They note that since 1994 'the number of people receiving social grants increased from 3 million to 16 million, benefitting the elderly, children and [military] veterans'. There follow three aims for the next five years: to train more social workers; to finalise policy discussions for a comprehensive social protection policy; and to 'continue to roll out existing social grants to those who qualify'. The reasons for this guarded and laconic approach to welfare are considered below.

The evolution of social protection policies before 1994

Chapter 2 described how the Pact and Fusion governments in the 1920s and 1930s sought to ameliorate white poverty by creating what was, for that period, a remarkably expansive set of welfare provisions. But the welfare benefits were highly racialised: Africans were ineligible for state pensions and a range of other grants and programmes. In 1939, when South Africa entered